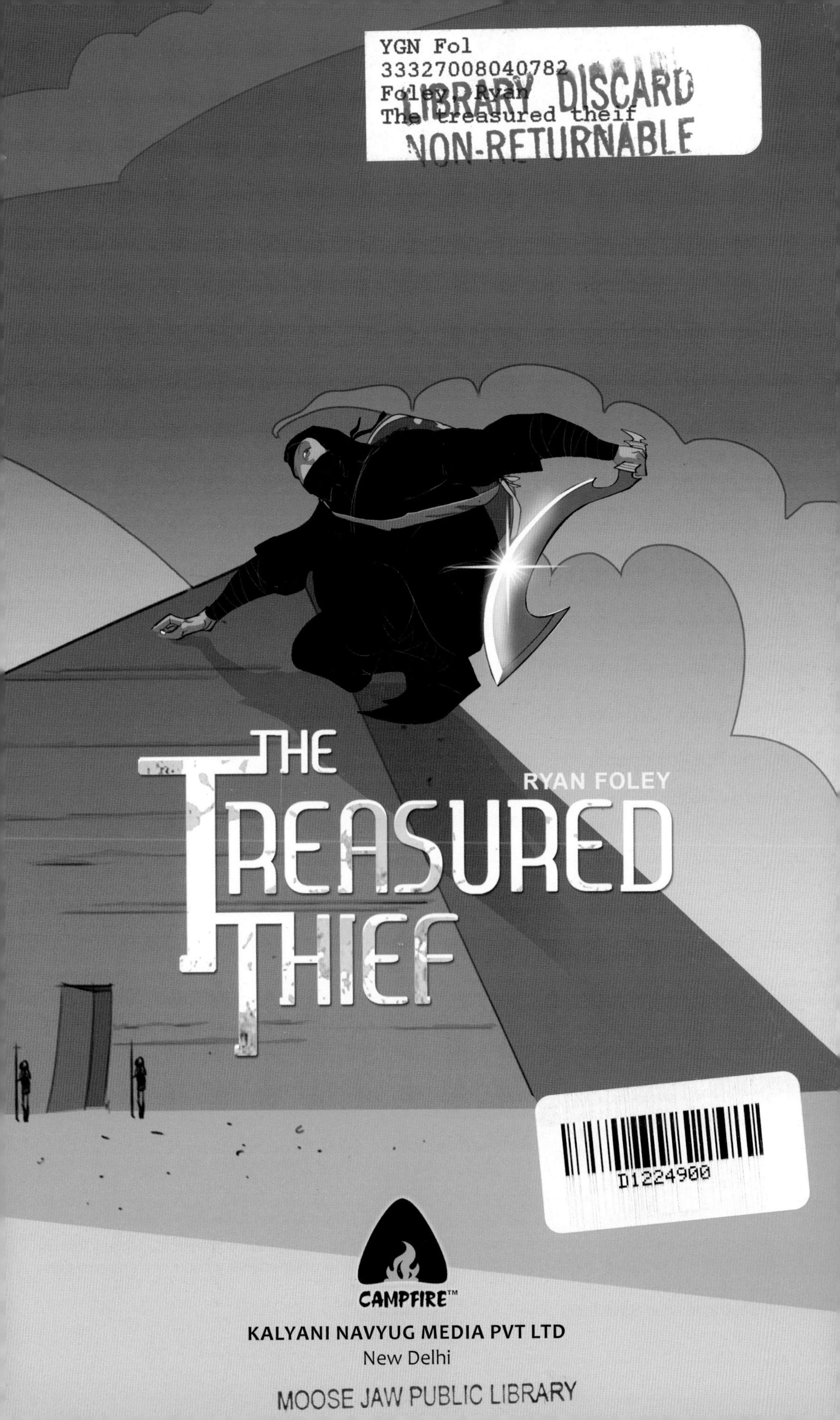

THE TREASURED THIEF

RYAN FOLEY

CAMPFIRE™
KALYANI NAVYUG MEDIA PVT LTD
New Delhi

THE TREASURED THIEF

RYAN FOLEY

Sitting around the Campfire, telling the story, were:

ILLUSTRATOR **SACHIN NAGAR**

COLORIST **PRADEEP SHERAWAT**

LETTERER **LAXMI CHAND GUPTA**

EDITOR **ASWATHY SENAN**

PRODUCTION CONTROLLER **VISHAL SHARMA**

COVER ART **SACHIN NAGAR**

DESIGNER **VIJAY SHARMA**

ART DIRECTOR **RAJESH NAGULAKONDA**

CAMPFIRE™

www.campfire.co.in

Published by Kalyani Navyug Media Pvt. Ltd.

101 C, Shiv House, Hari Nagar Ashram, New Delhi 110014, India

ISBN: 978-93-80741-11-6

Printed in India at Rave India

ABOUT THE AUTHOR

Born in 1974 in Toms River, New Jersey, Ryan Foley's obsession with comic books began during his childhood when his mother introduced him to characters like Spider-Man and Batman. He cites R. A. Salvatore's science fiction, *The Crystal Shard* (and its character Drizzt Do'Urden) as having influenced him the most, for it drew him into a world of fantasy and inspired him to become a writer. He has worked with Image Comics and Arcana Studios on comic book series such as *Masters of the Universe*, *Dragon's Lair*, *Space Ace*, and *Tales of Penance: Trial of the Century*.

Having adapted several Greek myths for Campfire, such as *Legend: The Labors of Heracles*, *Stolen Hearts: The Love of Eros and Psyche,* and *Perseus: Destiny's Call*, *The Treasured Thief* is Ryan's first foray into the rich and vibrant world of Egyptian legend.

ABOUT THE ARTIST

After completing his degree in computer applications, Sachin Nagar, a resident of New Delhi, India, strengthened his artistic skills by pursuing a diploma in animation, in which he made full use of his technological skills. A highly motivated artist, always seeking to excel, Sachin cites Michelangelo as his one great influence. *Photo Booth*, *The Call of the Wild*, and *Romeo and Juliet* are some of the titles he has illustrated for Campfire. His artwork for Campfire's Indian mythology title, *Ravana,* has won him great acclaim among critics and comic enthusiasts alike.

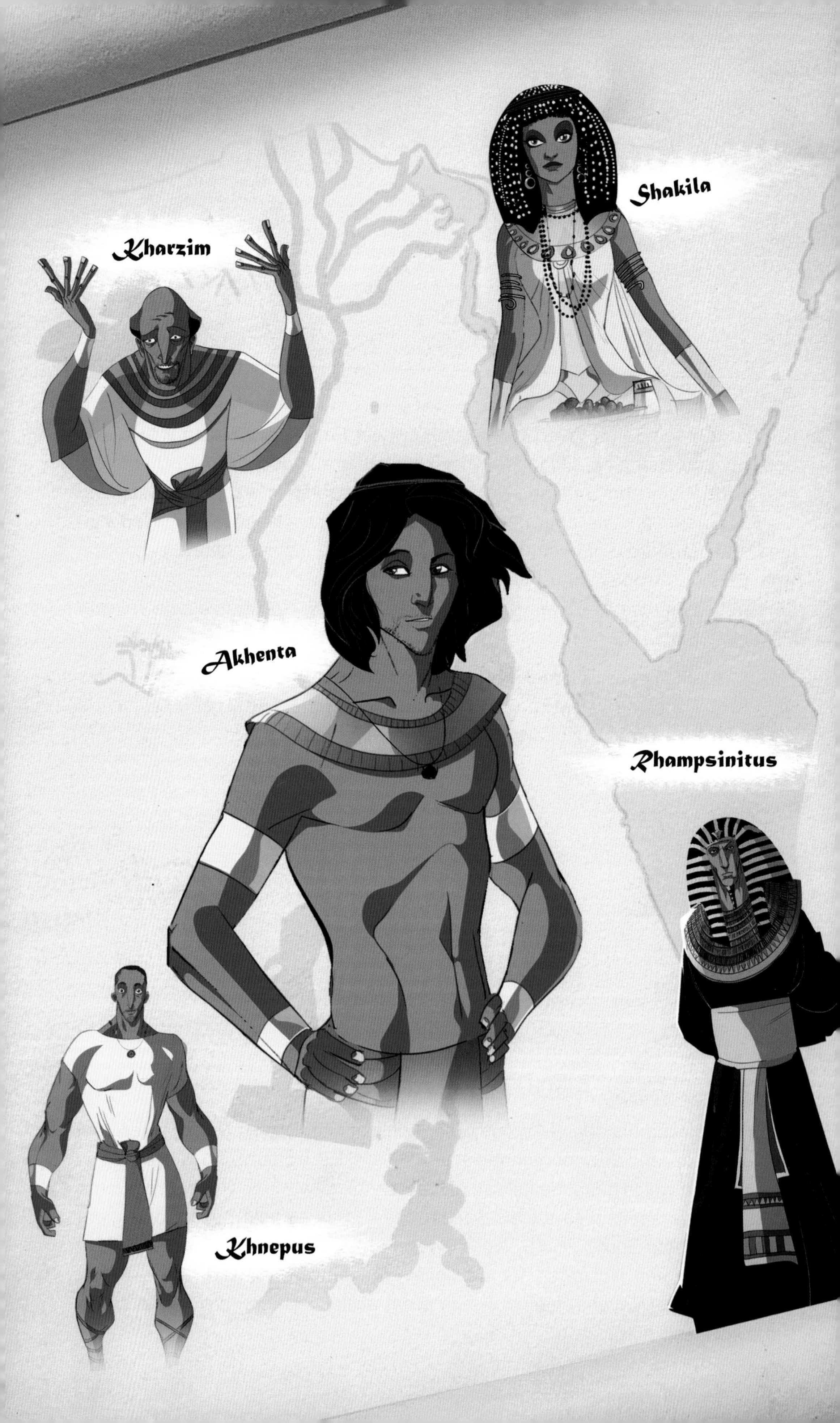
Kharzim
Shakila
Akhenta
Rhampsinitus
Khnepus

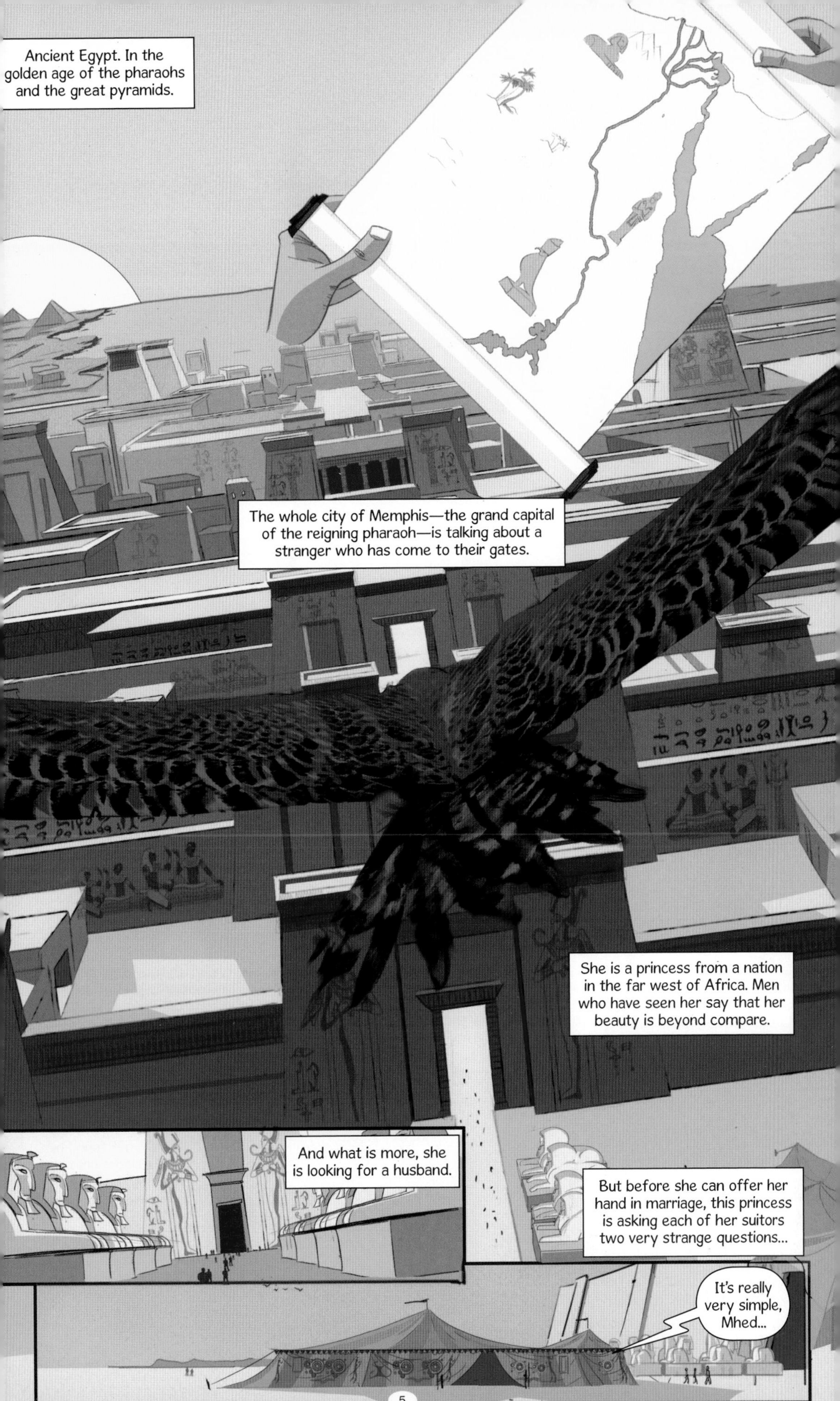
Ancient Egypt. In the golden age of the pharaohs and the great pyramids.
The whole city of Memphis—the grand capital of the reigning pharaoh—is talking about a stranger who has come to their gates.
She is a princess from a nation in the far west of Africa. Men who have seen her say that her beauty is beyond compare.
And what is more, she is looking for a husband.
But before she can offer her hand in marriage, this princess is asking each of her suitors two very strange questions...
It's really very simple, Mhed...

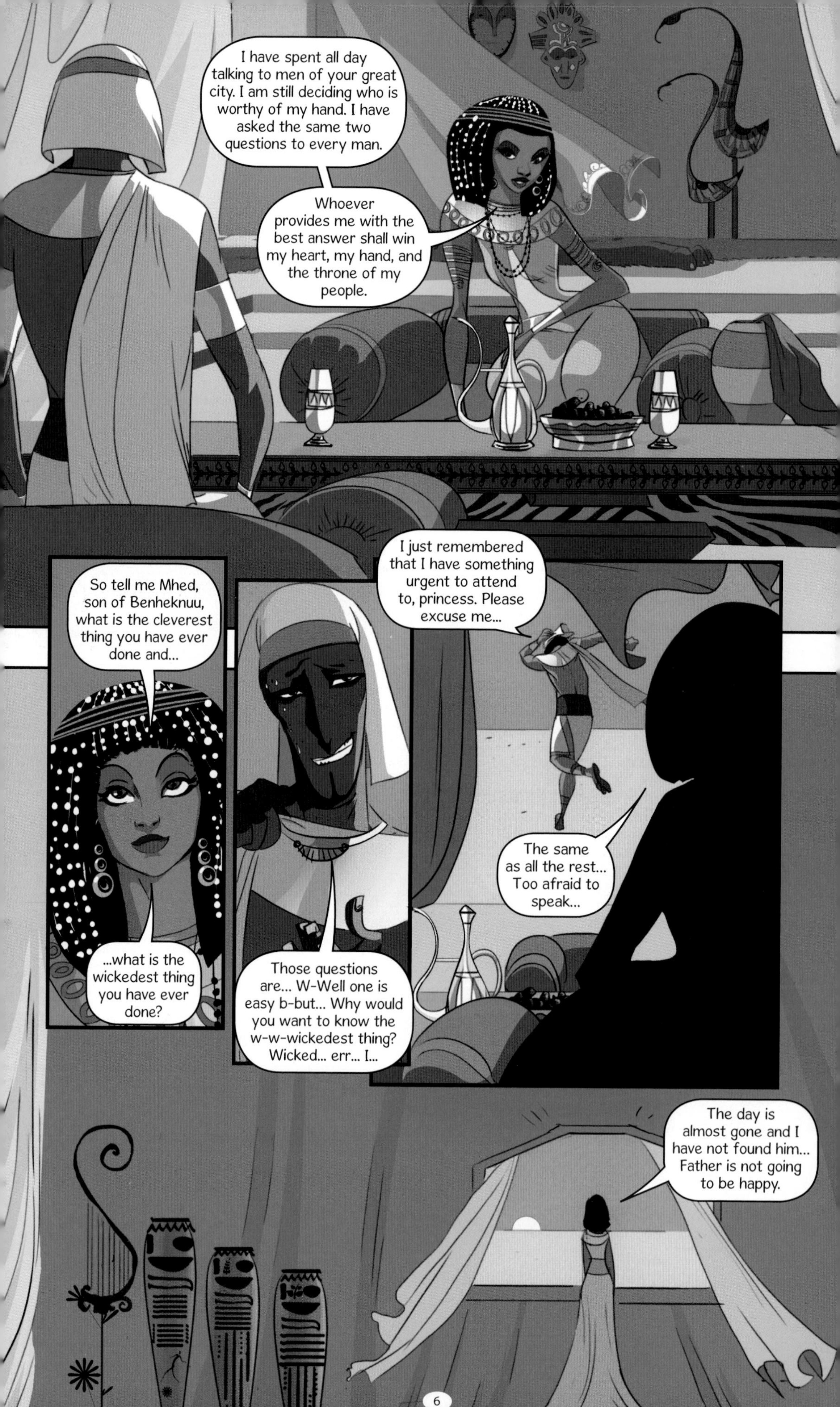
I have spent all day talking to men of your great city. I am still deciding who is worthy of my hand. I have asked the same two questions to every man.
Whoever provides me with the best answer shall win my heart, my hand, and the throne of my people.
So tell me Mhed, son of Benheknuu, what is the cleverest thing you have ever done and...
...what is the wickedest thing you have ever done?
Those questions are... W-Well one is easy b-but... Why would you want to know the w-w-wickedest thing? Wicked... err... I...
I just remembered that I have something urgent to attend to, princess. Please excuse me...
The same as all the rest... Too afraid to speak...
The day is almost gone and I have not found him... Father is not going to be happy.

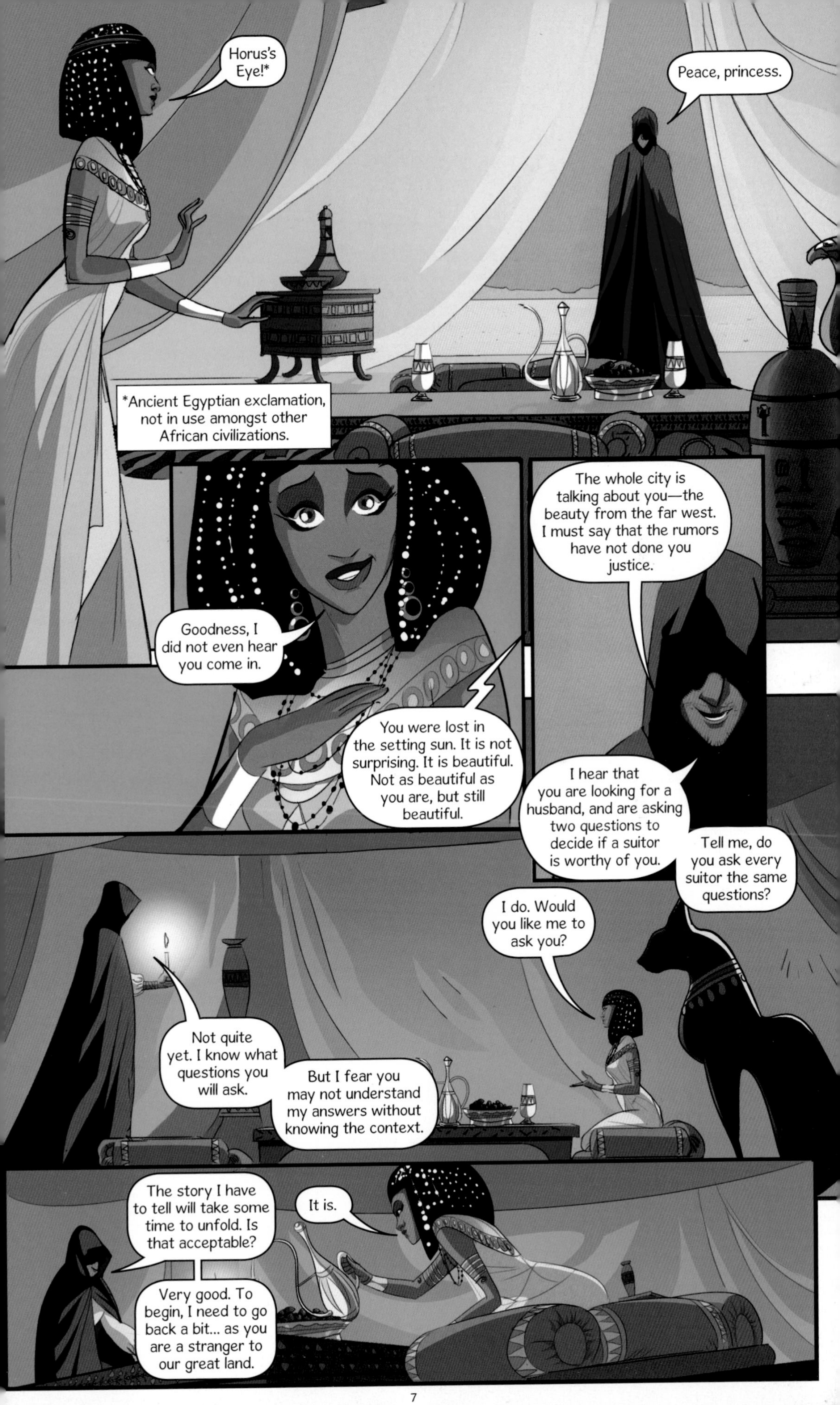
Horus's Eye!*
Peace, princess.
*Ancient Egyptian exclamation, not in use amongst other African civilizations.
Goodness, I did not even hear you come in.
You were lost in the setting sun. It is not surprising. It is beautiful. Not as beautiful as you are, but still beautiful.
The whole city is talking about you—the beauty from the far west. I must say that the rumors have not done you justice.
I hear that you are looking for a husband, and are asking two questions to decide if a suitor is worthy of you.
Tell me, do you ask every suitor the same questions?
I do. Would you like me to ask you?
Not quite yet. I know what questions you will ask.
But I fear you may not understand my answers without knowing the context.
The story I have to tell will take some time to unfold. Is that acceptable?
It is.
Very good. To begin, I need to go back a bit... as you are a stranger to our great land.

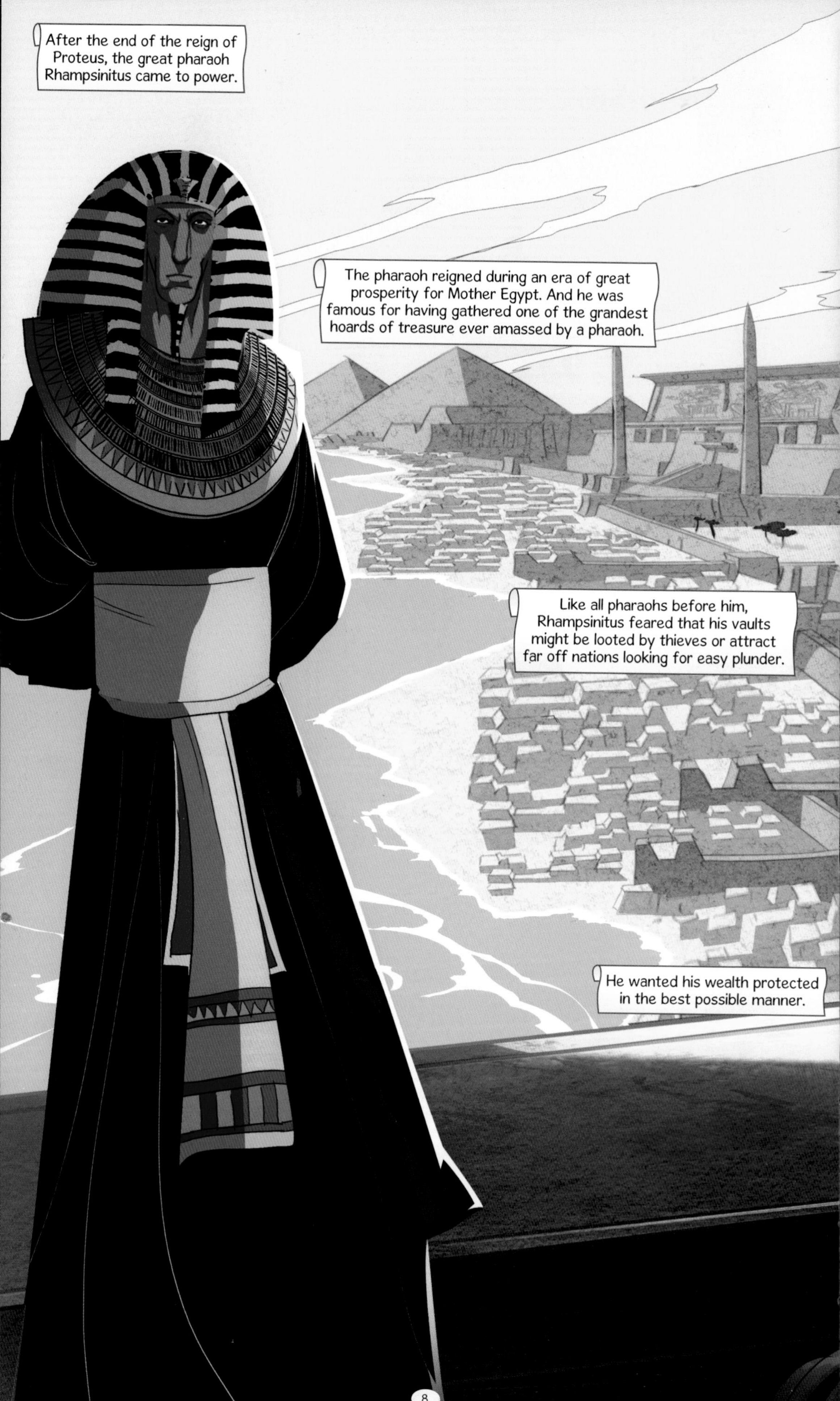
After the end of the reign of Proteus, the great pharaoh Rhampsinitus came to power.
The pharaoh reigned during an era of great prosperity for Mother Egypt. And he was famous for having gathered one of the grandest hoards of treasure ever amassed by a pharaoh.
Like all pharaohs before him, Rhampsinitus feared that his vaults might be looted by thieves or attract far off nations looking for easy plunder.
He wanted his wealth protected in the best possible manner.

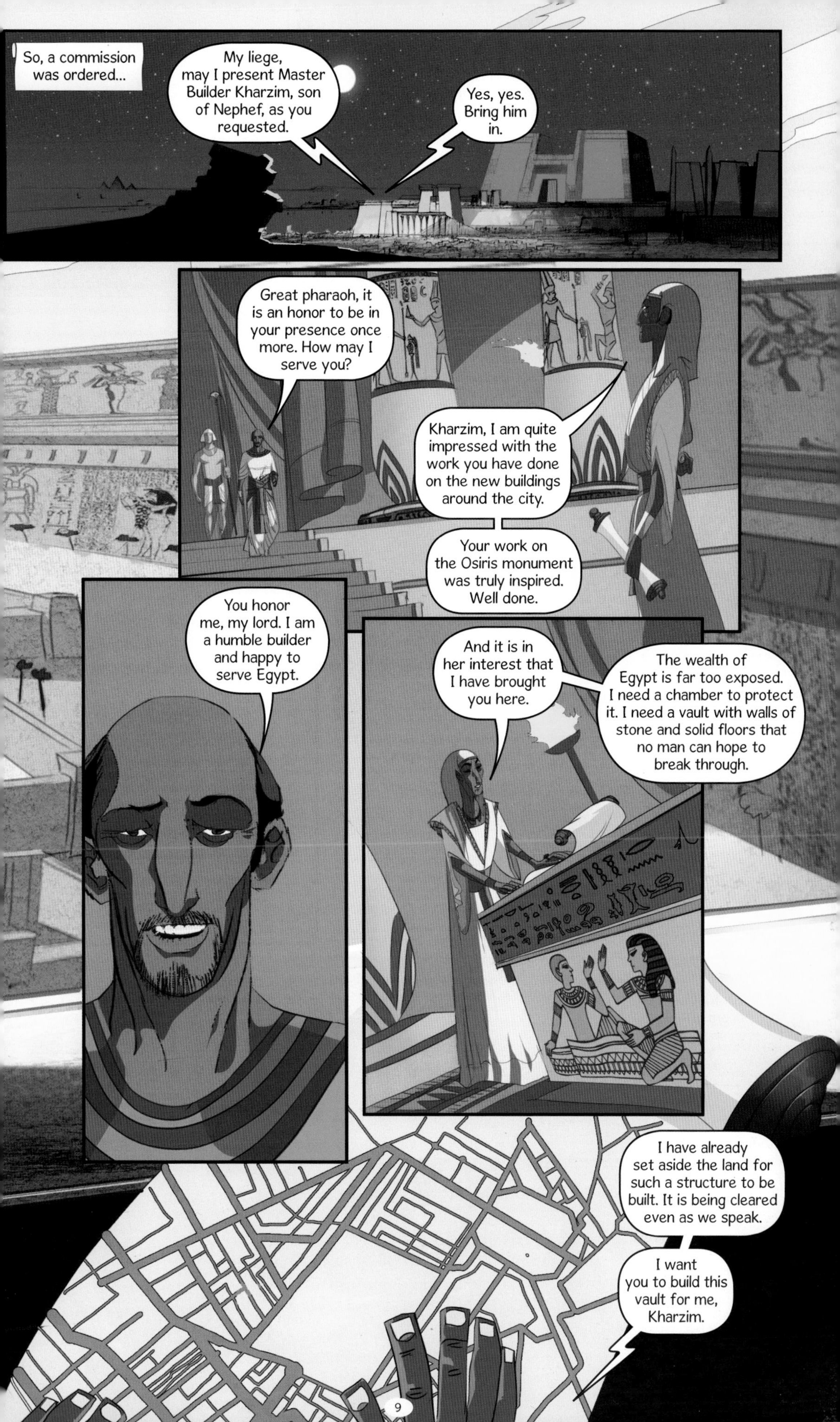

So, a commission was ordered...
My liege, may I present Master Builder Kharzim, son of Nephef, as you requested.
Yes, yes. Bring him in.
Great pharaoh, it is an honor to be in your presence once more. How may I serve you?
Kharzim, I am quite impressed with the work you have done on the new buildings around the city.
Your work on the Osiris monument was truly inspired. Well done.
You honor me, my lord. I am a humble builder and happy to serve Egypt.
And it is in her interest that I have brought you here.
The wealth of Egypt is far too exposed. I need a chamber to protect it. I need a vault with walls of stone and solid floors that no man can hope to break through.
I have already set aside the land for such a structure to be built. It is being cleared even as we speak.
I want you to build this vault for me, Kharzim.

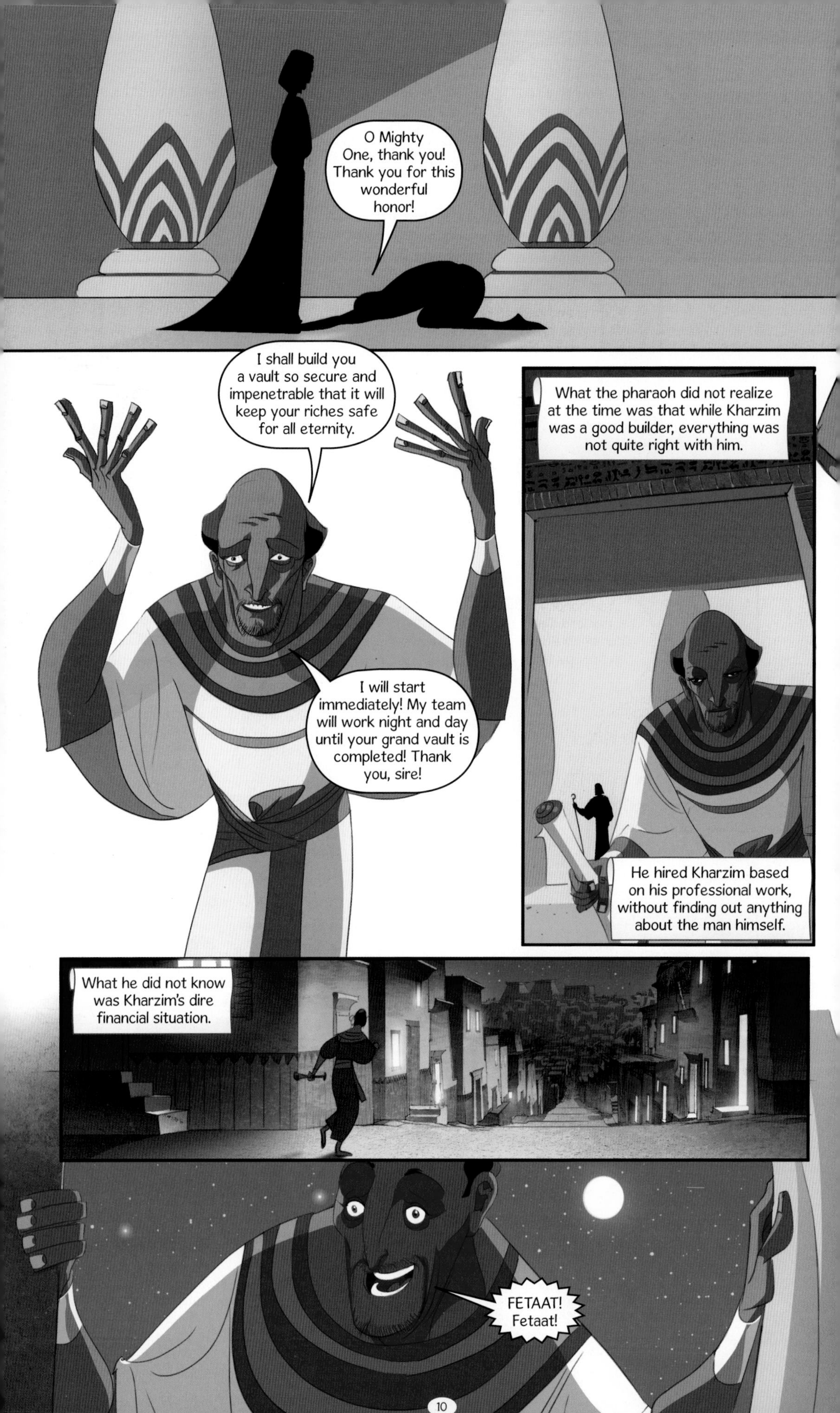
O Mighty One, thank you! Thank you for this wonderful honor!
I shall build you a vault so secure and impenetrable that it will keep your riches safe for all eternity.
I will start immediately! My team will work night and day until your grand vault is completed! Thank you, sire!
What the pharaoh did not realize at the time was that while Kharzim was a good builder, everything was not quite right with him.
He hired Kharzim based on his professional work, without finding out anything about the man himself.
What he did not know was Kharzim's dire financial situation.
FETAAT! Fetaat!

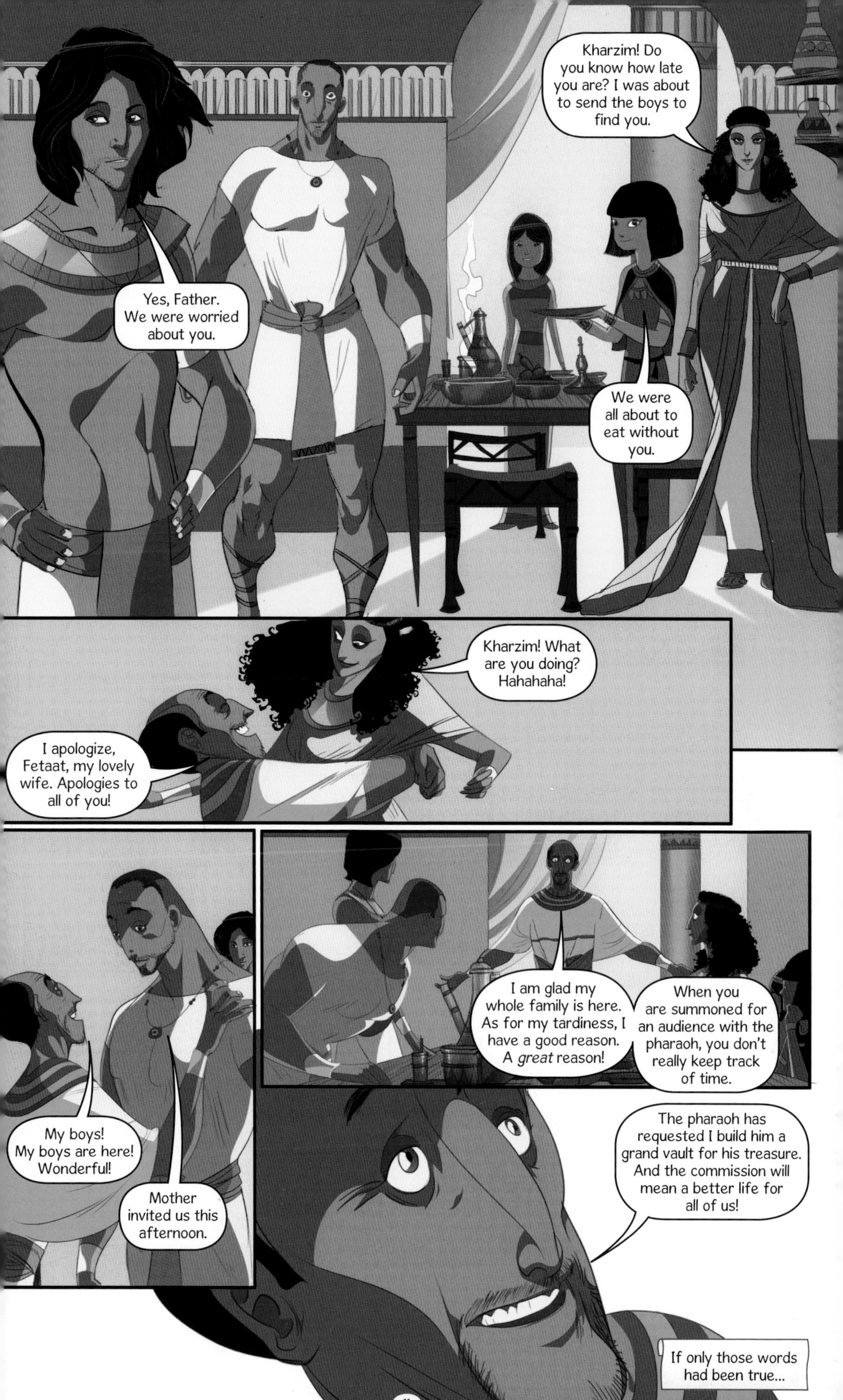
Kharzim! Do you know how late you are? I was about to send the boys to find you.
Yes, Father. We were worried about you.
We were all about to eat without you.
Kharzim! What are you doing? Hahahaha!
I apologize, Fetaat, my lovely wife. Apologies to all of you!
My boys! My boys are here! Wonderful!
Mother invited us this afternoon.
I am glad my whole family is here. As for my tardiness, I have a good reason. A *great* reason!
When you are summoned for an audience with the pharaoh, you don't really keep track of time.
The pharaoh has requested I build him a grand vault for his treasure. And the commission will mean a better life for all of us!
If only those words had been true...

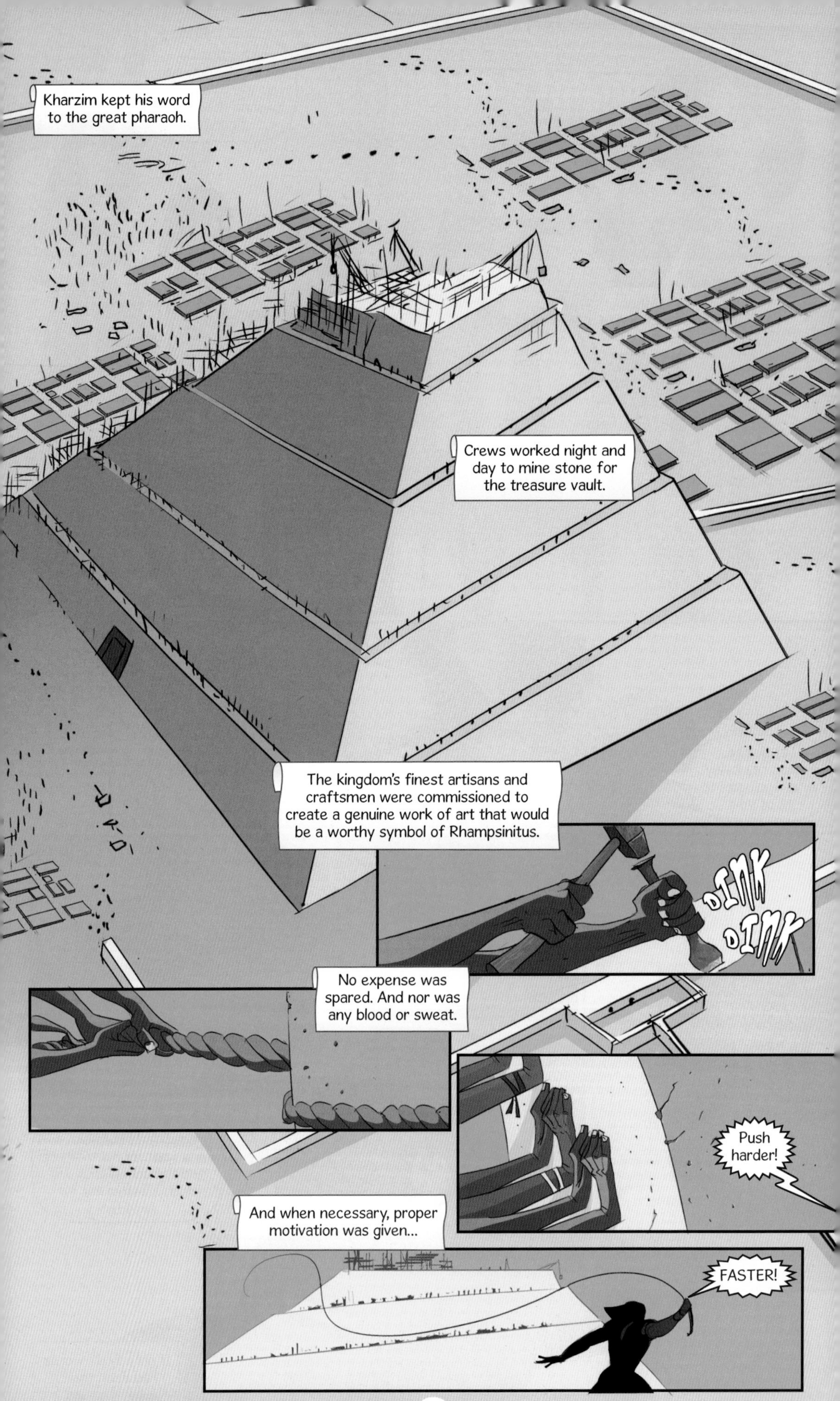

Kharzim kept his word to the great pharaoh.
Crews worked night and day to mine stone for the treasure vault.
The kingdom's finest artisans and craftsmen were commissioned to create a genuine work of art that would be a worthy symbol of Rhampsinitus.
DINK DINK
No expense was spared. And nor was any blood or sweat.
Push harder!
And when necessary, proper motivation was given...
FASTER!

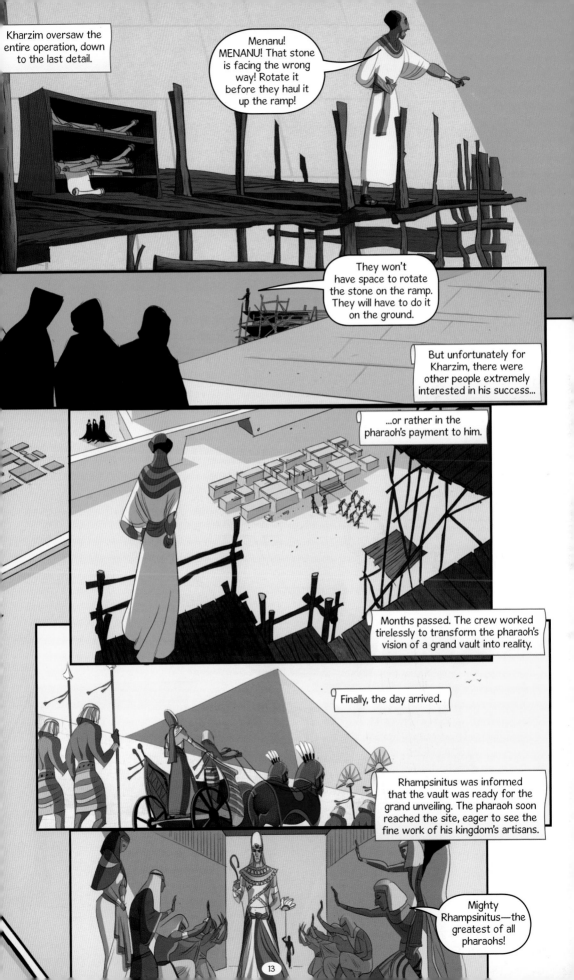

Kharzim oversaw the entire operation, down to the last detail.

Menanu! MENANU! That stone is facing the wrong way! Rotate it before they haul it up the ramp!

They won't have space to rotate the stone on the ramp. They will have to do it on the ground.

But unfortunately for Kharzim, there were other people extremely interested in his success...

...or rather in the pharaoh's payment to him.

Months passed. The crew worked tirelessly to transform the pharaoh's vision of a grand vault into reality.

Finally, the day arrived.

Rhampsinitus was informed that the vault was ready for the grand unveiling. The pharaoh soon reached the site, eager to see the fine work of his kingdom's artisans.

Mighty Rhampsinitus—the greatest of all pharaohs!

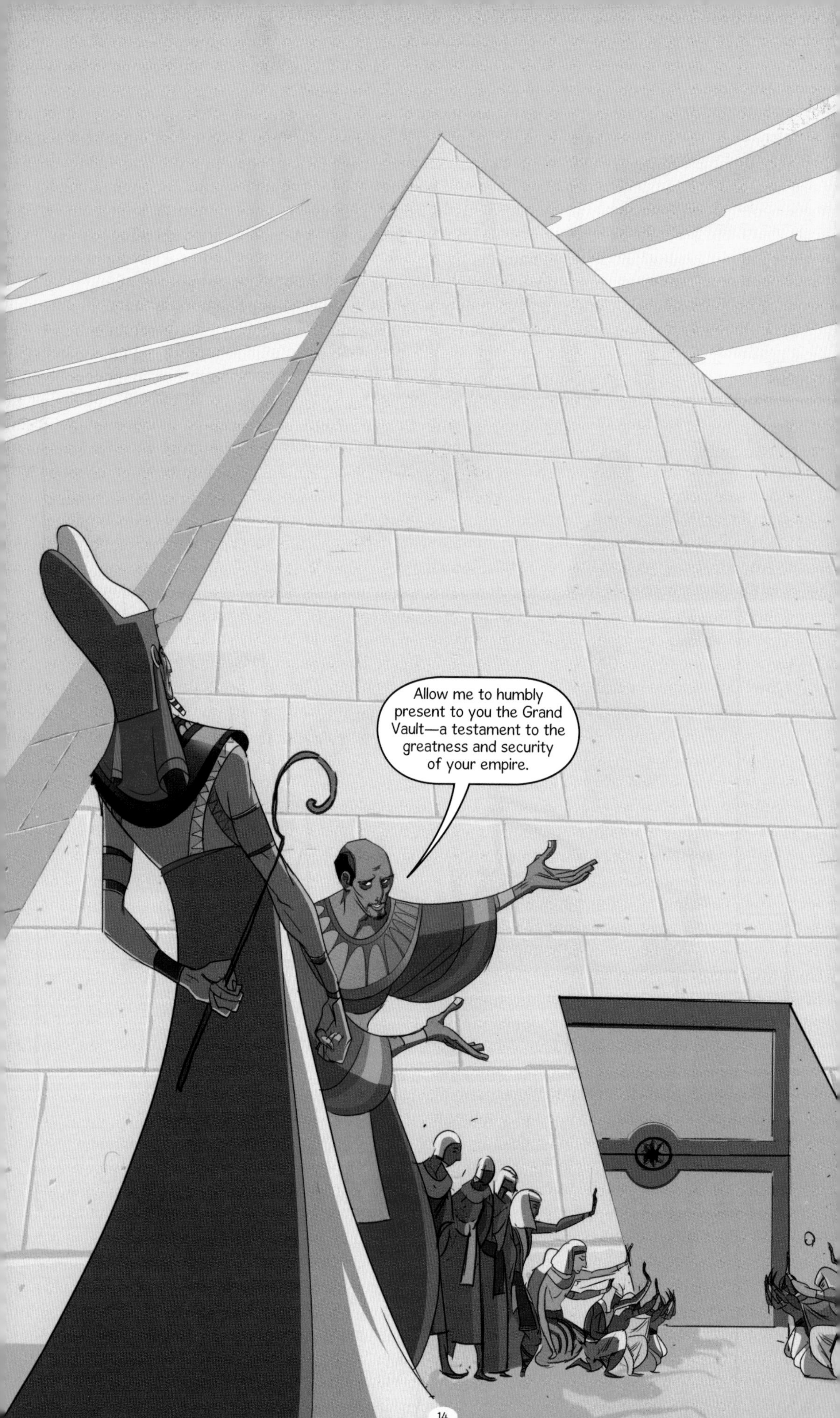
Allow me to humbly present to you the Grand Vault—a testament to the greatness and security of your empire.

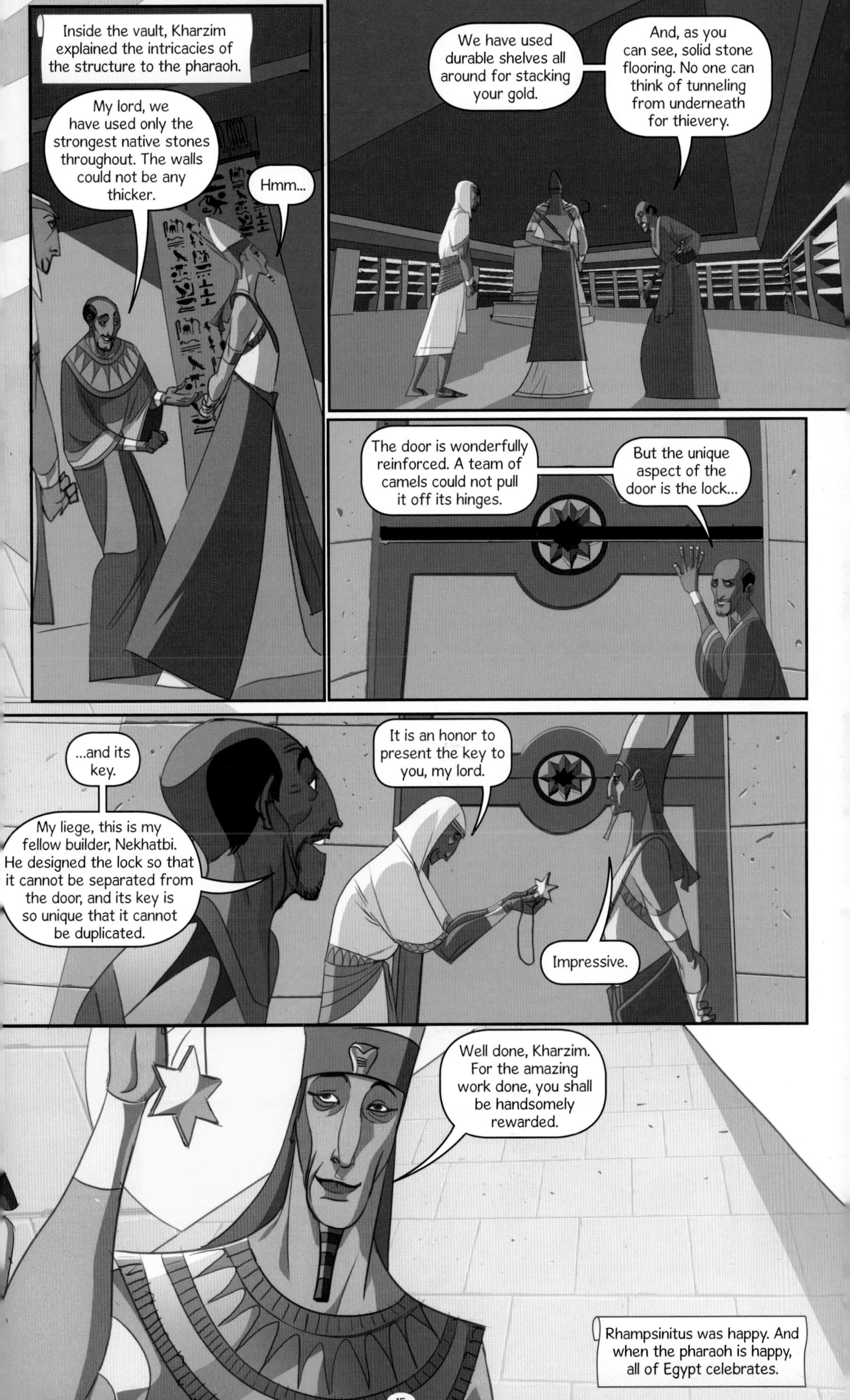
Inside the vault, Kharzim explained the intricacies of the structure to the pharaoh.
My lord, we have used only the strongest native stones throughout. The walls could not be any thicker.
Hmm...
We have used durable shelves all around for stacking your gold.
And, as you can see, solid stone flooring. No one can think of tunneling from underneath for thievery.
The door is wonderfully reinforced. A team of camels could not pull it off its hinges.
But the unique aspect of the door is the lock...
...and its key.
My liege, this is my fellow builder, Nekhatbi. He designed the lock so that it cannot be separated from the door, and its key is so unique that it cannot be duplicated.
It is an honor to present the key to you, my lord.
Impressive.
Well done, Kharzim. For the amazing work done, you shall be handsomely rewarded.
Rhampsinitus was happy. And when the pharaoh is happy, all of Egypt celebrates.

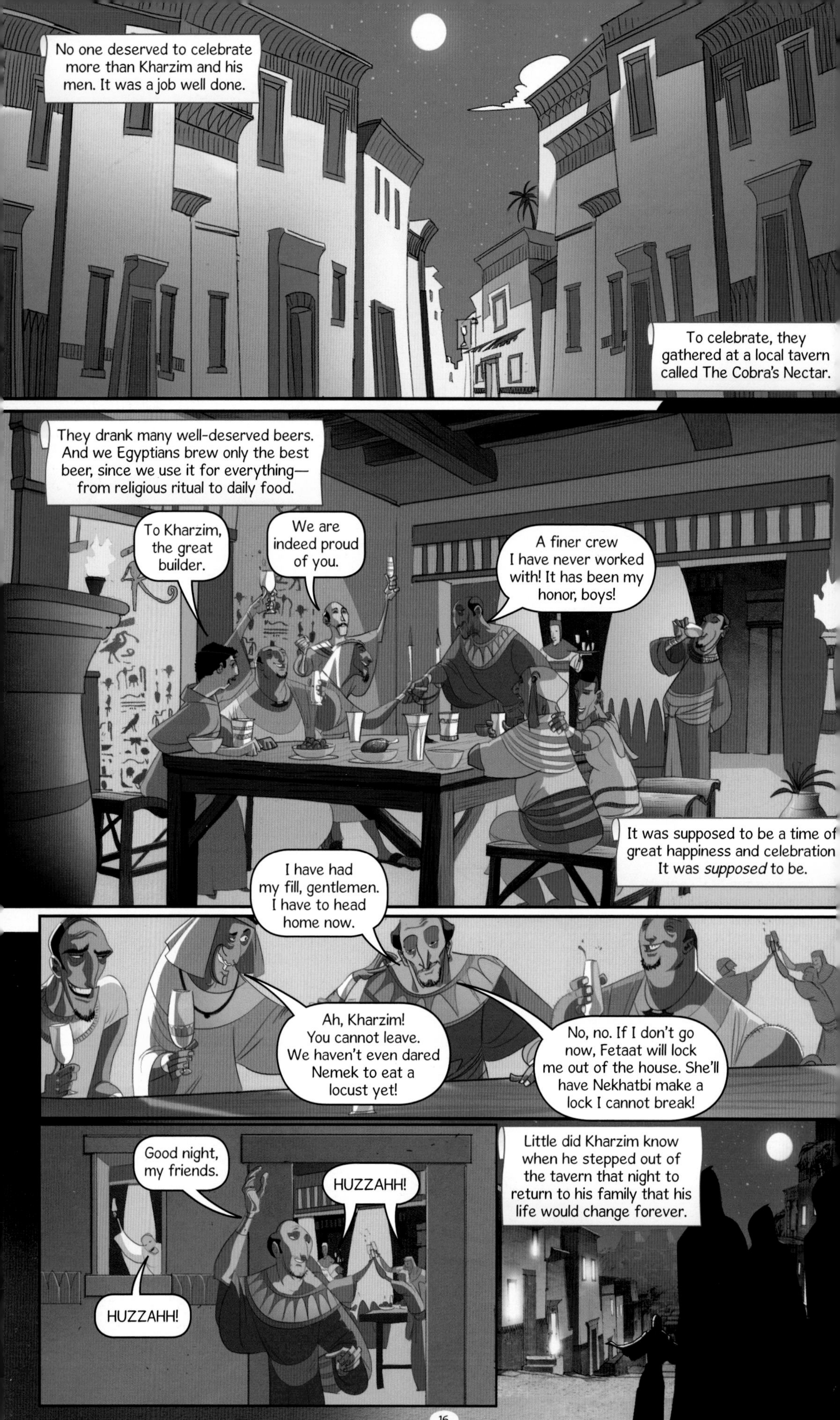

No one deserved to celebrate more than Kharzim and his men. It was a job well done.
To celebrate, they gathered at a local tavern called The Cobra's Nectar.
They drank many well-deserved beers. And we Egyptians brew only the best beer, since we use it for everything—from religious ritual to daily food.
To Kharzim, the great builder.
We are indeed proud of you.
A finer crew I have never worked with! It has been my honor, boys!
It was supposed to be a time of great happiness and celebration It was *supposed* to be.
I have had my fill, gentlemen. I have to head home now.
Ah, Kharzim! You cannot leave. We haven't even dared Nemek to eat a locust yet!
No, no. If I don't go now, Fetaat will lock me out of the house. She'll have Nekhatbi make a lock I cannot break!
Good night, my friends.
HUZZAHH!
HUZZAHH!
Little did Kharzim know when he stepped out of the tavern that night to return to his family that his life would change forever.

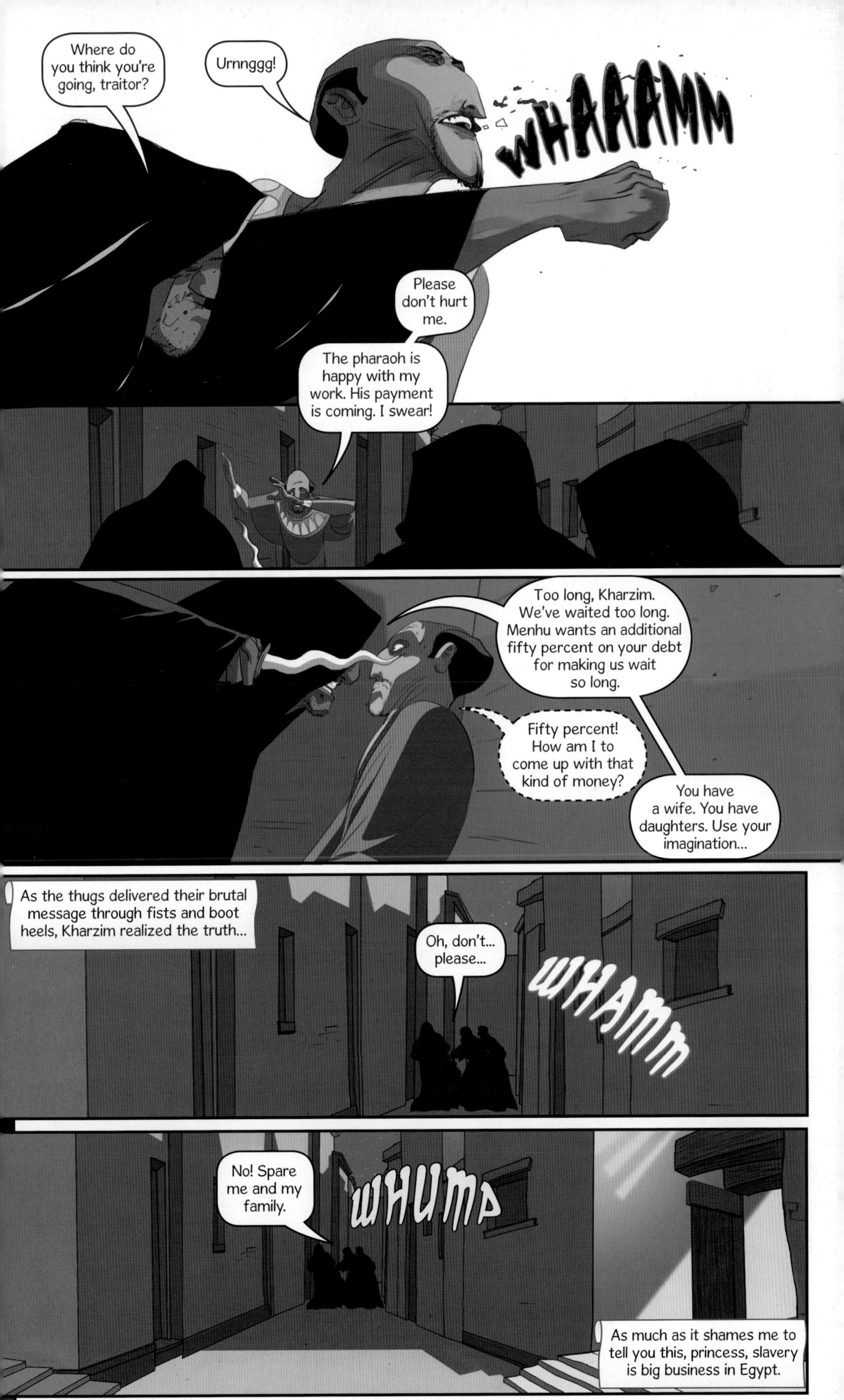
Where do you think you're going, traitor?
Urnnggg!
WHAAAMM
Please don't hurt me.
The pharaoh is happy with my work. His payment is coming. I swear!
Too long, Kharzim. We've waited too long. Menhu wants an additional fifty percent on your debt for making us wait so long.
Fifty percent! How am I to come up with that kind of money?
You have a wife. You have daughters. Use your imagination...
As the thugs delivered their brutal message through fists and boot heels, Kharzim realized the truth...
Oh, don't... please...
WHAMM
No! Spare me and my family.
WHUMP
As much as it shames me to tell you this, princess, slavery is big business in Egypt.

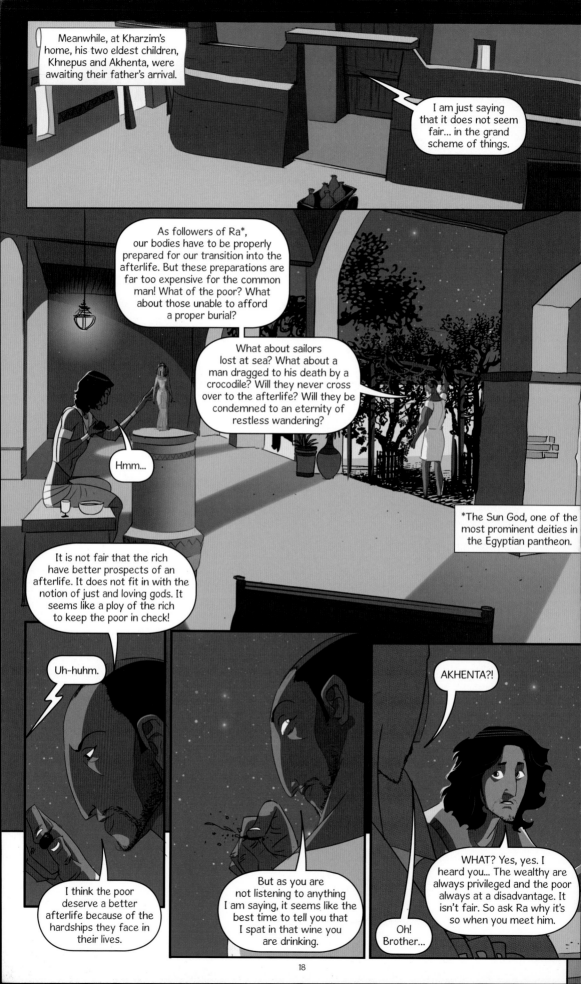

Meanwhile, at Kharzim's home, his two eldest children, Khnepus and Akhenta, were awaiting their father's arrival.

I am just saying that it does not seem fair... in the grand scheme of things.

As followers of Ra*, our bodies have to be properly prepared for our transition into the afterlife. But these preparations are far too expensive for the common man! What of the poor? What about those unable to afford a proper burial?

What about sailors lost at sea? What about a man dragged to his death by a crocodile? Will they never cross over to the afterlife? Will they be condemned to an eternity of restless wandering?

Hmm...

*The Sun God, one of the most prominent deities in the Egyptian pantheon.

It is not fair that the rich have better prospects of an afterlife. It does not fit in with the notion of just and loving gods. It seems like a ploy of the rich to keep the poor in check!

Uh-huhm.

AKHENTA?!

I think the poor deserve a better afterlife because of the hardships they face in their lives.

But as you are not listening to anything I am saying, it seems like the best time to tell you that I spat in that wine you are drinking.

Oh! Brother...

WHAT? Yes, yes. I heard you... The wealthy are always privileged and the poor always at a disadvantage. It isn't fair. So ask Ra why it's so when you meet him.

18

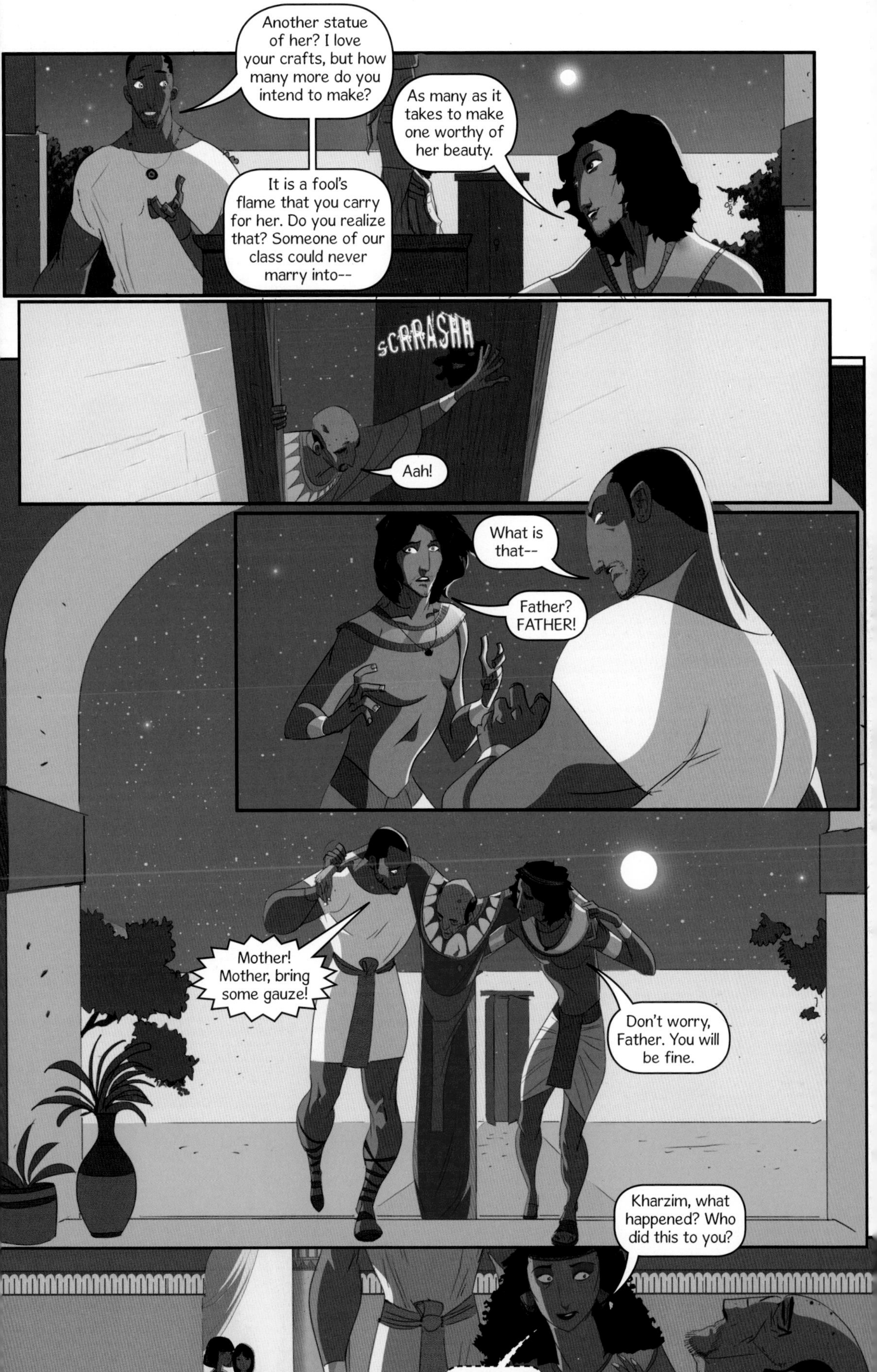

Another statue of her? I love your crafts, but how many more do you intend to make?
It is a fool's flame that you carry for her. Do you realize that? Someone of our class could never marry into--
As many as it takes to make one worthy of her beauty.
SCRRASHH
Aah!
What is that--
Father? FATHER!
Mother! Mother, bring some gauze!
Don't worry, Father. You will be fine.
Kharzim, what happened? Who did this to you?
It was them, wasn't it?

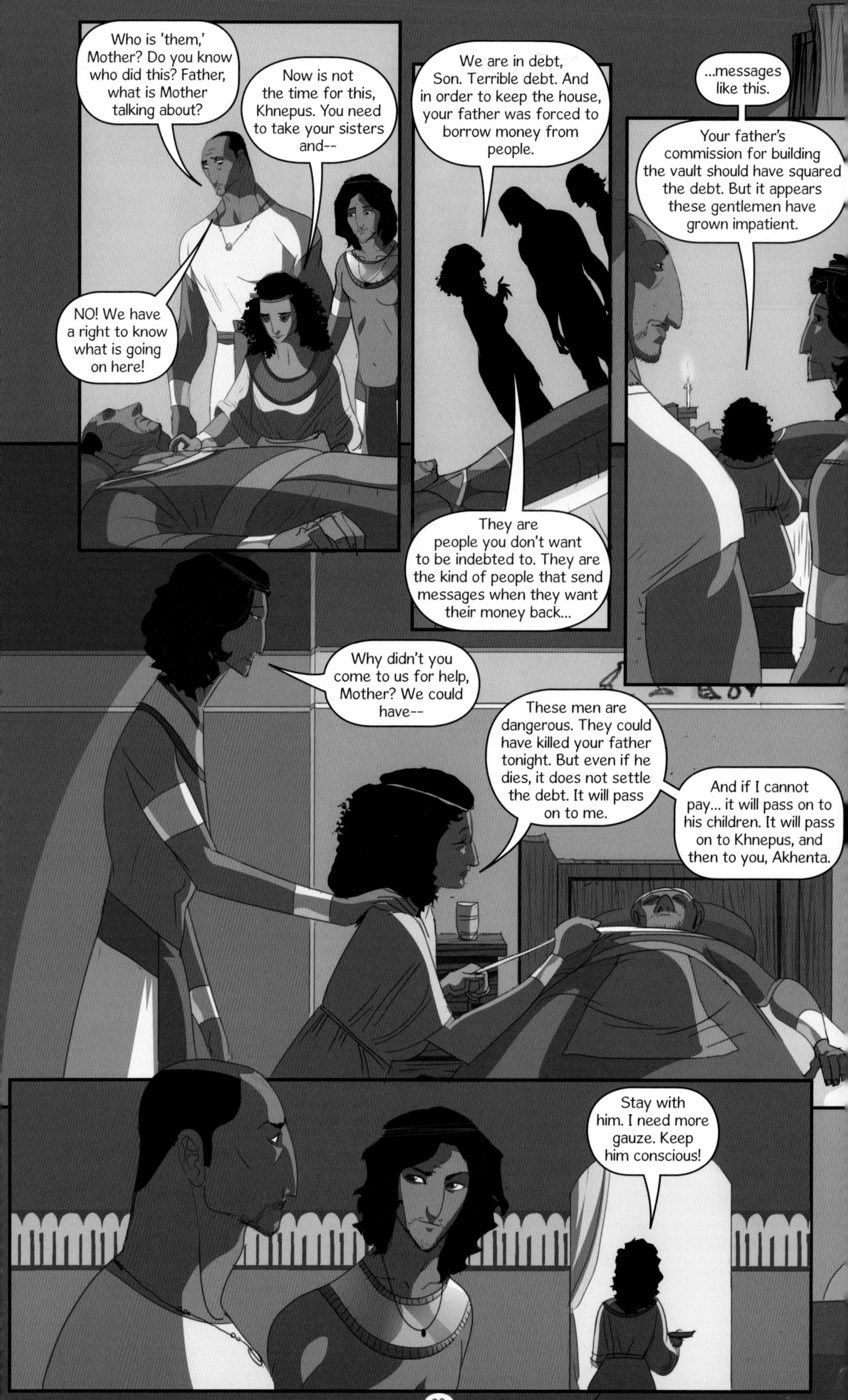

Who is 'them,' Mother? Do you know who did this? Father, what is Mother talking about?
Now is not the time for this, Khnepus. You need to take your sisters and--
NO! We have a right to know what is going on here!
We are in debt, Son. Terrible debt. And in order to keep the house, your father was forced to borrow money from people.
They are people you don't want to be indebted to. They are the kind of people that send messages when they want their money back...
...messages like this.
Your father's commission for building the vault should have squared the debt. But it appears these gentlemen have grown impatient.
Why didn't you come to us for help, Mother? We could have--
These men are dangerous. They could have killed your father tonight. But even if he dies, it does not settle the debt. It will pass on to me.
And if I cannot pay... it will pass on to his children. It will pass on to Khnepus, and then to you, Akhenta.
Stay with him. I need more gauze. Keep him conscious!

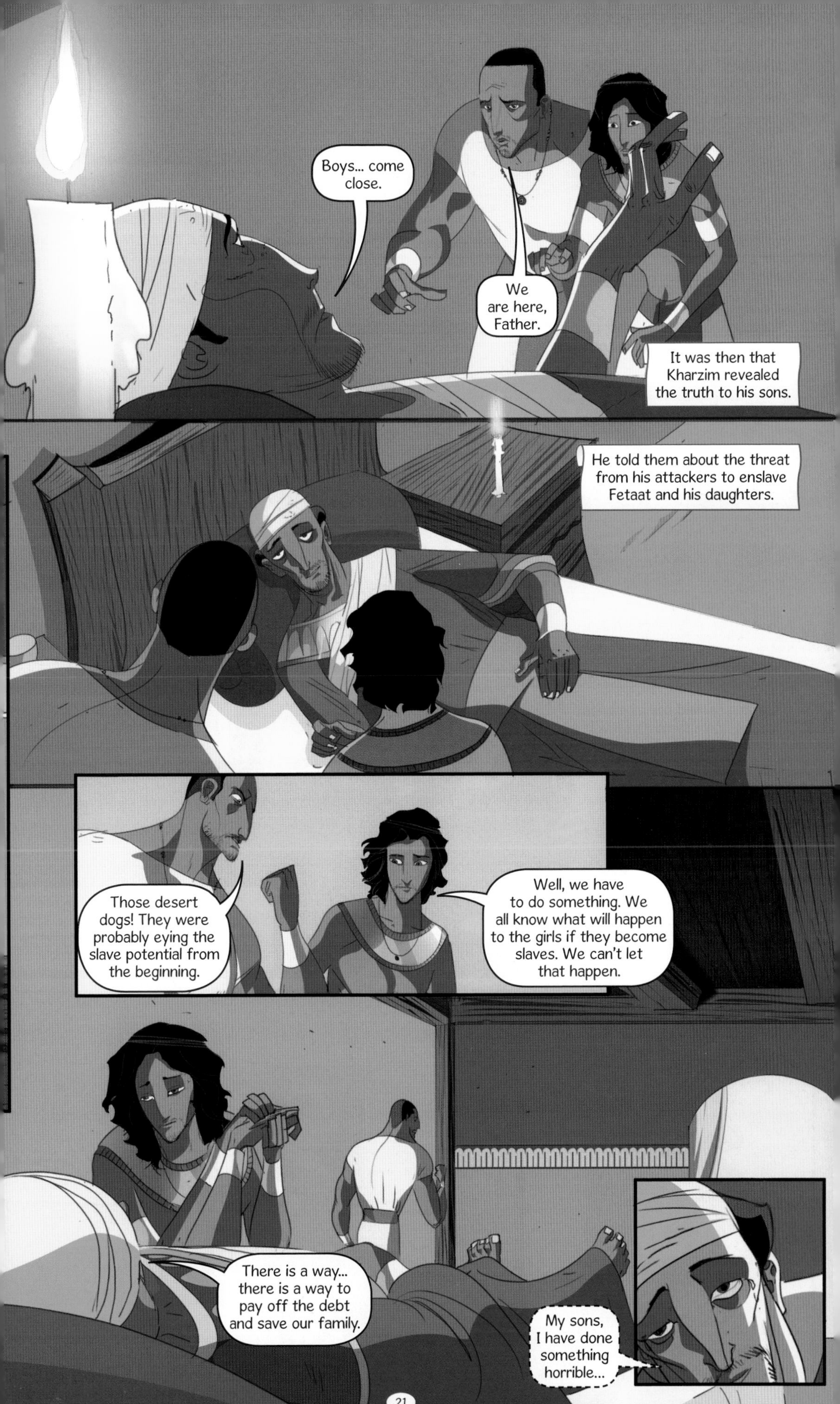
Boys... come close.
We are here, Father.
It was then that Kharzim revealed the truth to his sons.
He told them about the threat from his attackers to enslave Fetaat and his daughters.
Those desert dogs! They were probably eying the slave potential from the beginning.
Well, we have to do something. We all know what will happen to the girls if they become slaves. We can't let that happen.
There is a way... there is a way to pay off the debt and save our family.
My sons, I have done something horrible...

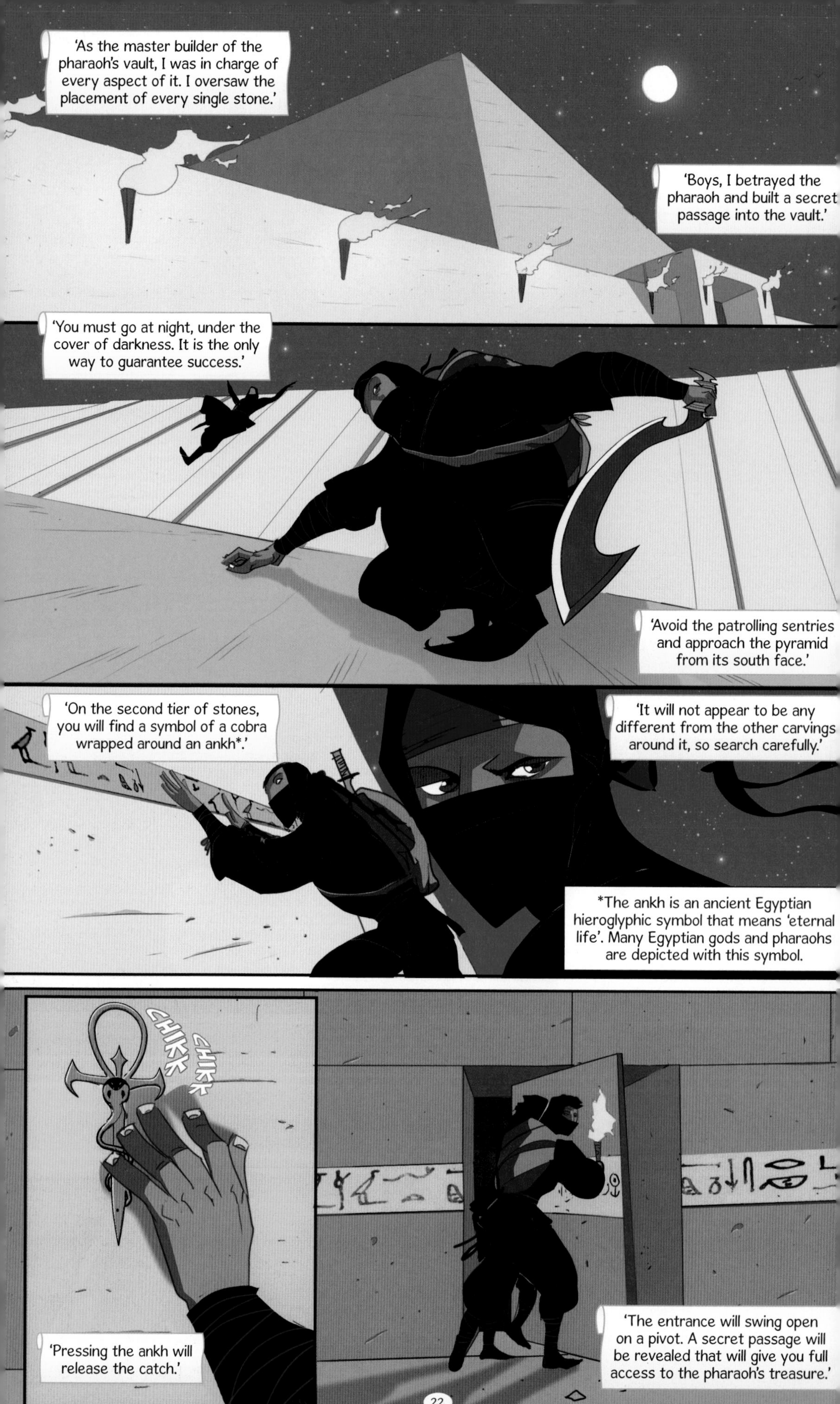
'As the master builder of the pharaoh's vault, I was in charge of every aspect of it. I oversaw the placement of every single stone.'
'Boys, I betrayed the pharaoh and built a secret passage into the vault.'
'You must go at night, under the cover of darkness. It is the only way to guarantee success.'
'Avoid the patrolling sentries and approach the pyramid from its south face.'
'On the second tier of stones, you will find a symbol of a cobra wrapped around an ankh*.'
'It will not appear to be any different from the other carvings around it, so search carefully.'
*The ankh is an ancient Egyptian hieroglyphic symbol that means 'eternal life'. Many Egyptian gods and pharaohs are depicted with this symbol.
CHIKK
CHIKK
'Pressing the ankh will release the catch.'
'The entrance will swing open on a pivot. A secret passage will be revealed that will give you full access to the pharaoh's treasure.'

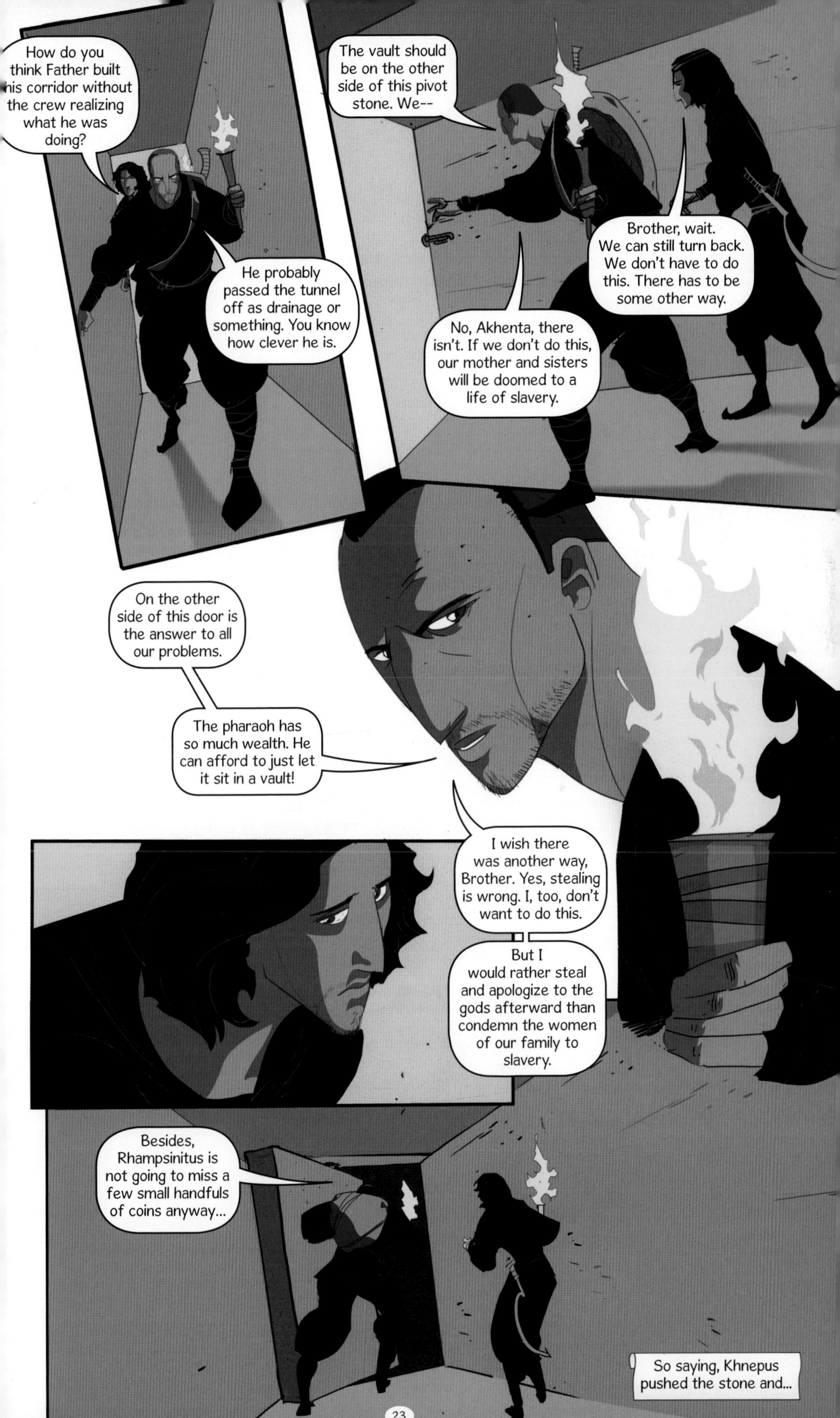

How do you think Father built his corridor without the crew realizing what he was doing?
He probably passed the tunnel off as drainage or something. You know how clever he is.
The vault should be on the other side of this pivot stone. We--
Brother, wait. We can still turn back. We don't have to do this. There has to be some other way.
No, Akhenta, there isn't. If we don't do this, our mother and sisters will be doomed to a life of slavery.
On the other side of this door is the answer to all our problems.
The pharaoh has so much wealth. He can afford to just let it sit in a vault!
I wish there was another way, Brother. Yes, stealing is wrong. I, too, don't want to do this.
But I would rather steal and apologize to the gods afterward than condemn the women of our family to slavery.
Besides, Rhampsinitus is not going to miss a few small handfuls of coins anyway...
So saying, Khnepus pushed the stone and...

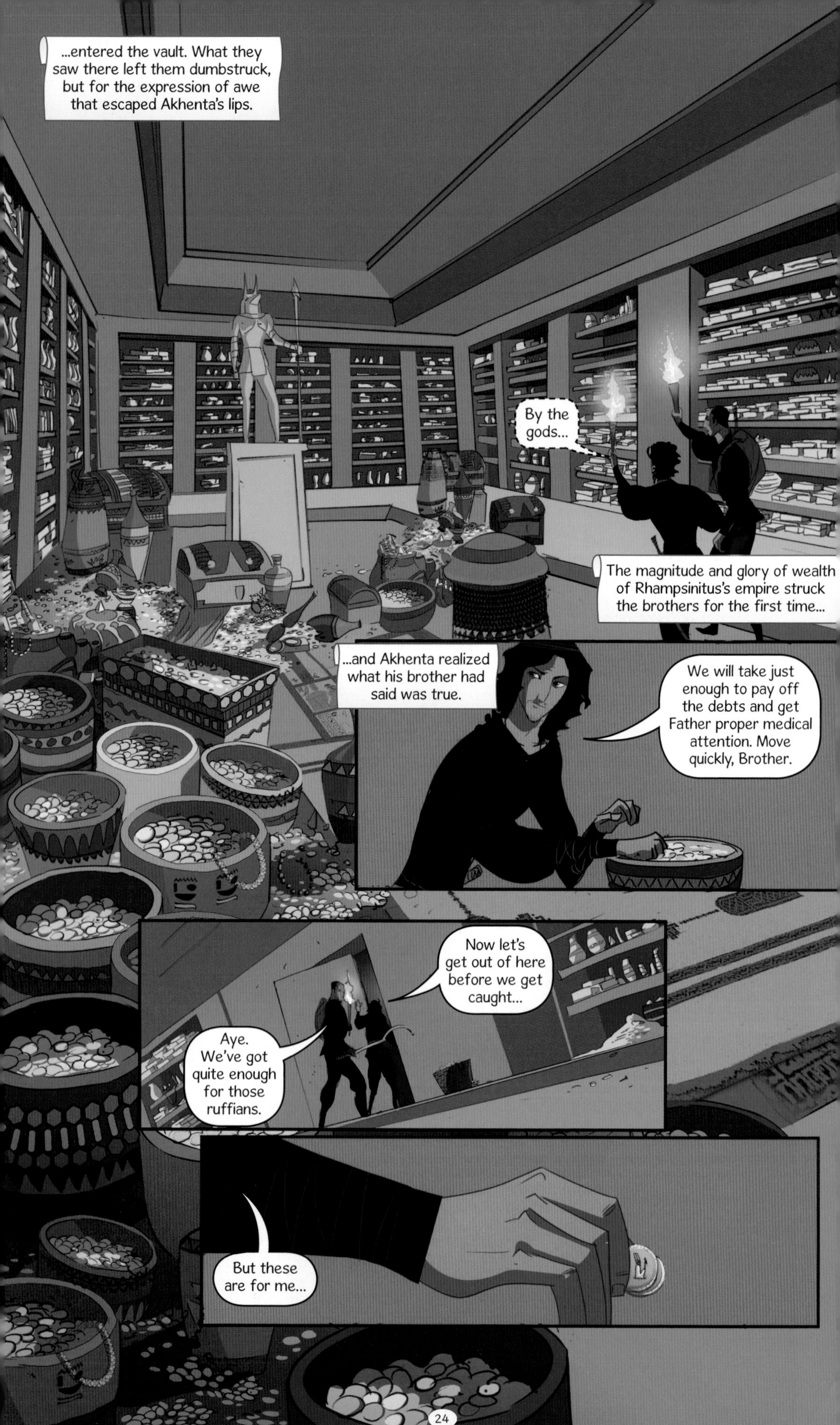
...entered the vault. What they saw there left them dumbstruck, but for the expression of awe that escaped Akhenta's lips.
By the gods...
The magnitude and glory of wealth of Rhampsinitus's empire struck the brothers for the first time...
...and Akhenta realized what his brother had said was true.
We will take just enough to pay off the debts and get Father proper medical attention. Move quickly, Brother.
Now let's get out of here before we get caught...
Aye. We've got quite enough for those ruffians.
But these are for me...

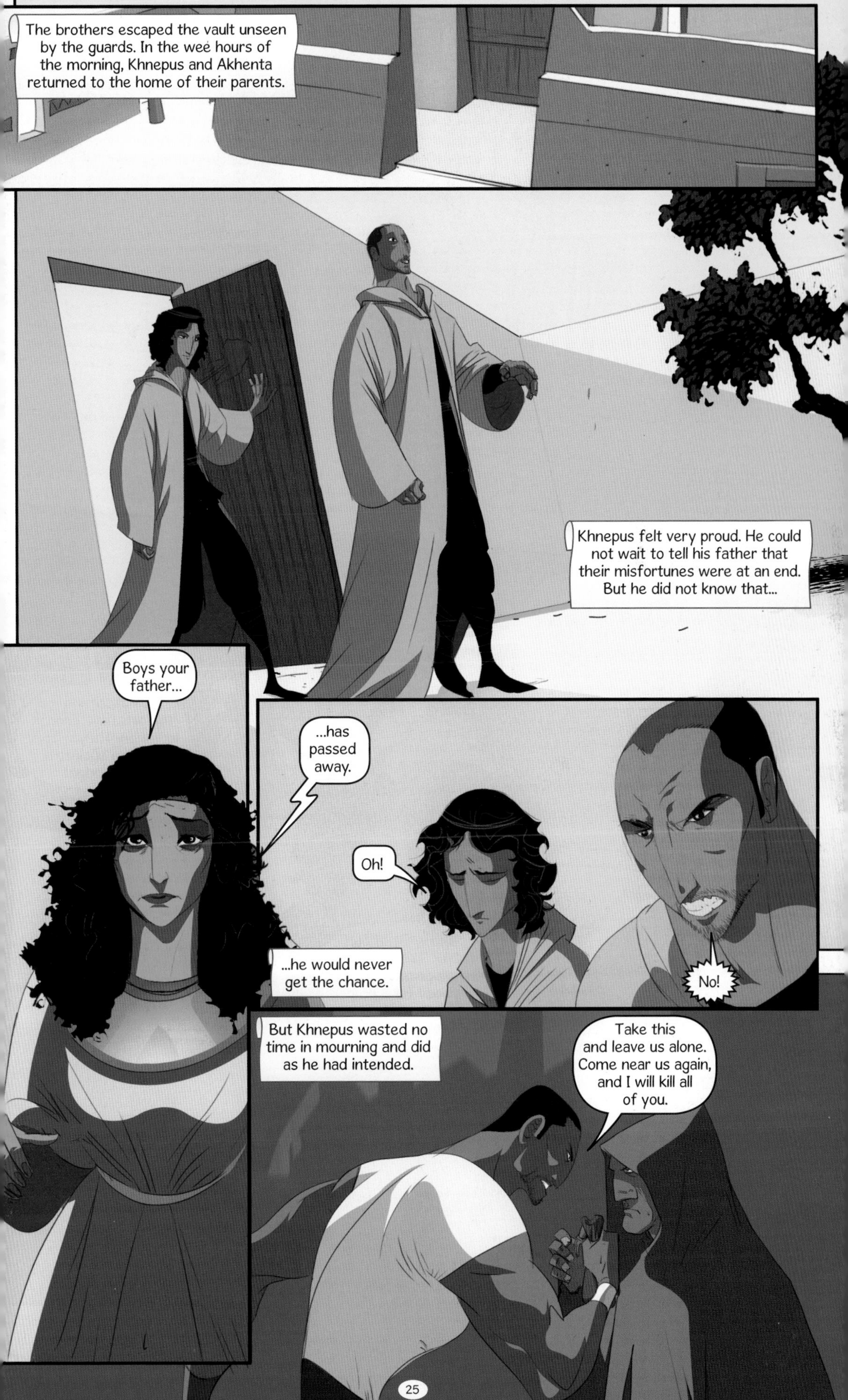

The brothers escaped the vault unseen by the guards. In the wee hours of the morning, Khnepus and Akhenta returned to the home of their parents.
Khnepus felt very proud. He could not wait to tell his father that their misfortunes were at an end. But he did not know that...
Boys your father...
...has passed away.
Oh!
...he would never get the chance.
No!
But Khnepus wasted no time in mourning and did as he had intended.
Take this and leave us alone. Come near us again, and I will kill all of you.

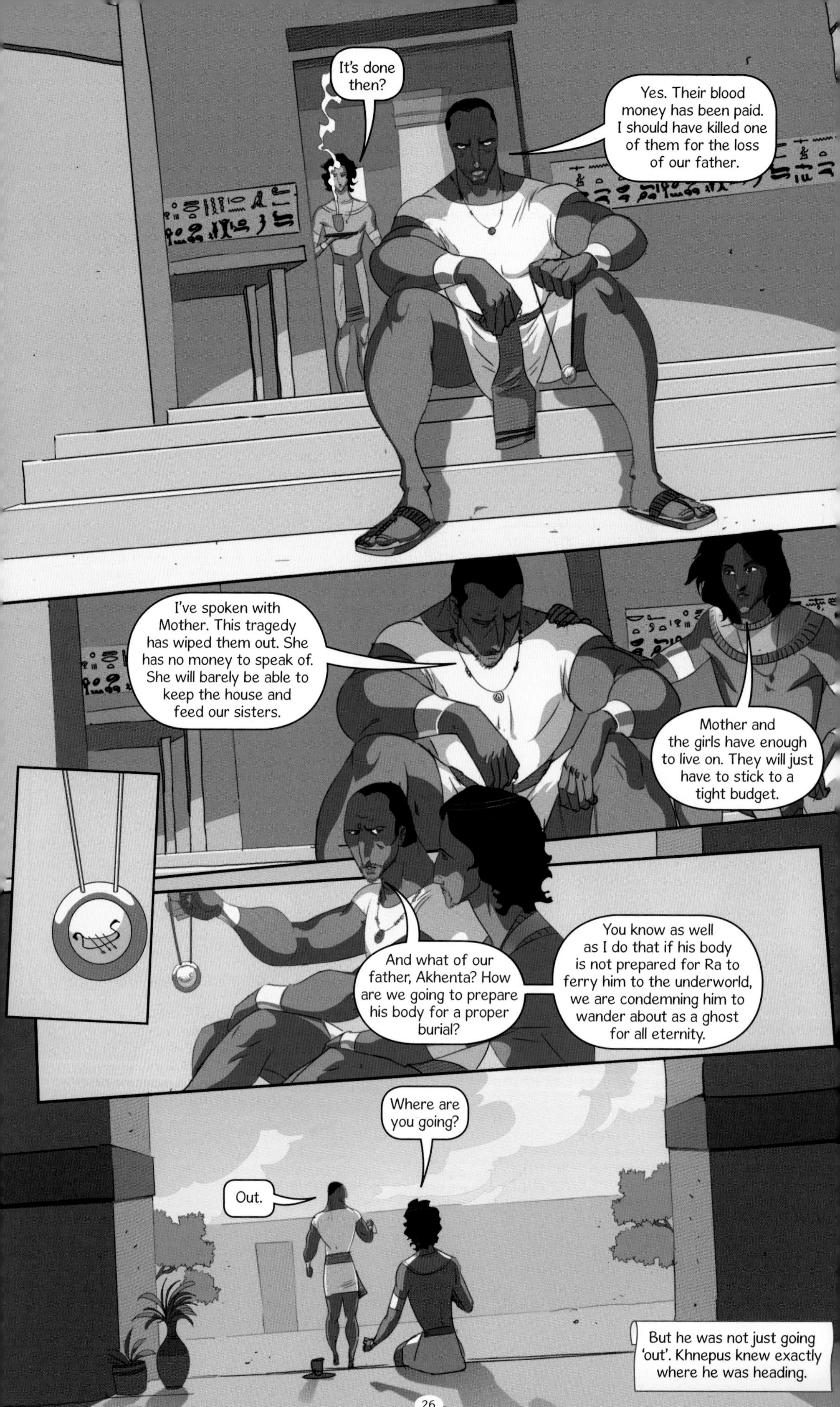

It's done then?
Yes. Their blood money has been paid. I should have killed one of them for the loss of our father.
I've spoken with Mother. This tragedy has wiped them out. She has no money to speak of. She will barely be able to keep the house and feed our sisters.
Mother and the girls have enough to live on. They will just have to stick to a tight budget.
And what of our father, Akhenta? How are we going to prepare his body for a proper burial?
You know as well as I do that if his body is not prepared for Ra to ferry him to the underworld, we are condemning him to wander about as a ghost for all eternity.
Where are you going?
Out.
But he was not just going 'out'. Khnepus knew exactly where he was heading.

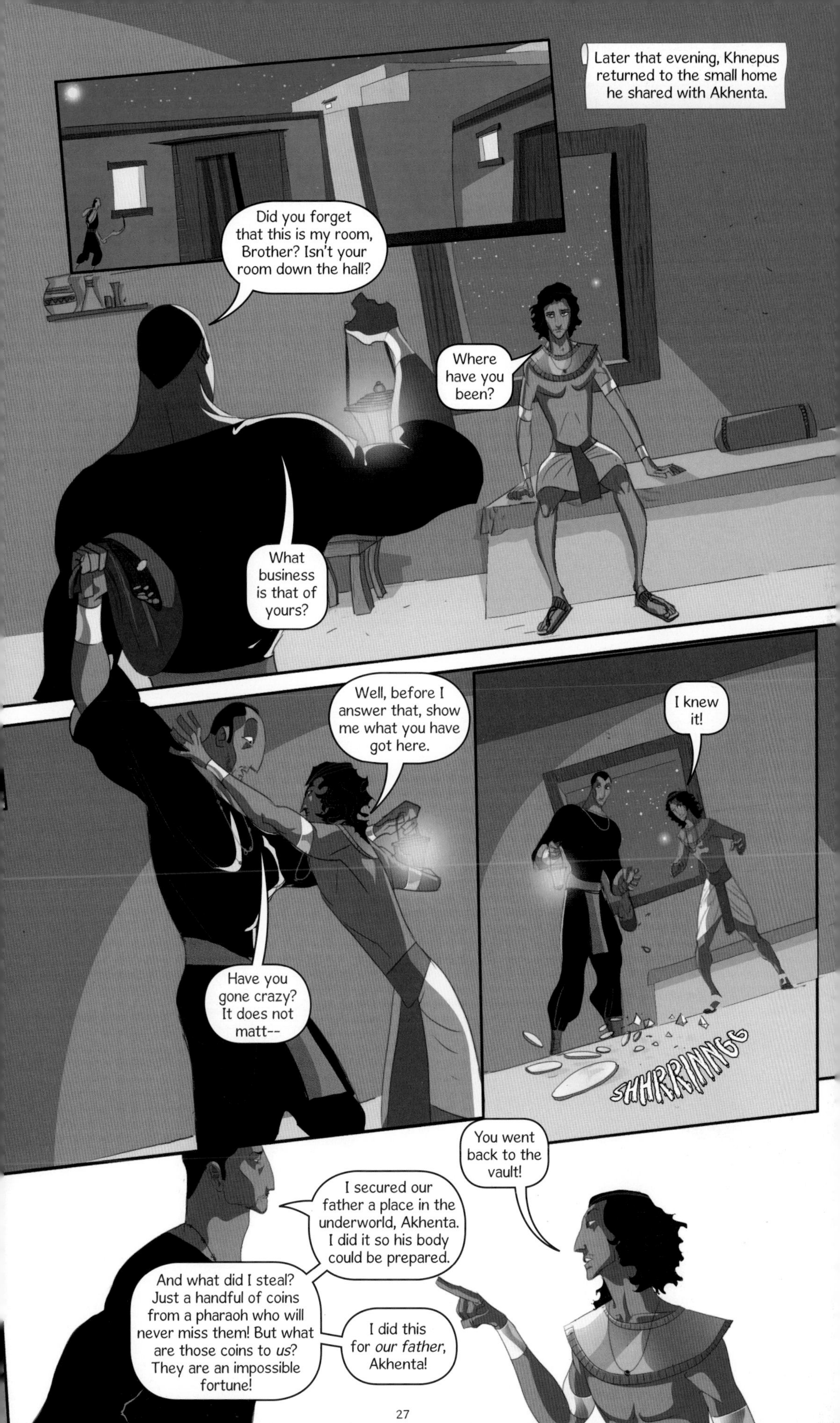
Later that evening, Khnepus returned to the small home he shared with Akhenta.
Did you forget that this is my room, Brother? Isn't your room down the hall?
Where have you been?
What business is that of yours?
Well, before I answer that, show me what you have got here.
Have you gone crazy? It does not matt--
I knew it!
SHHRRINNGG
You went back to the vault!
I secured our father a place in the underworld, Akhenta. I did it so his body could be prepared.
And what did I steal? Just a handful of coins from a pharaoh who will never miss them! But what are those coins to *us*? They are an impossible fortune!
I did this for *our father*, Akhenta!

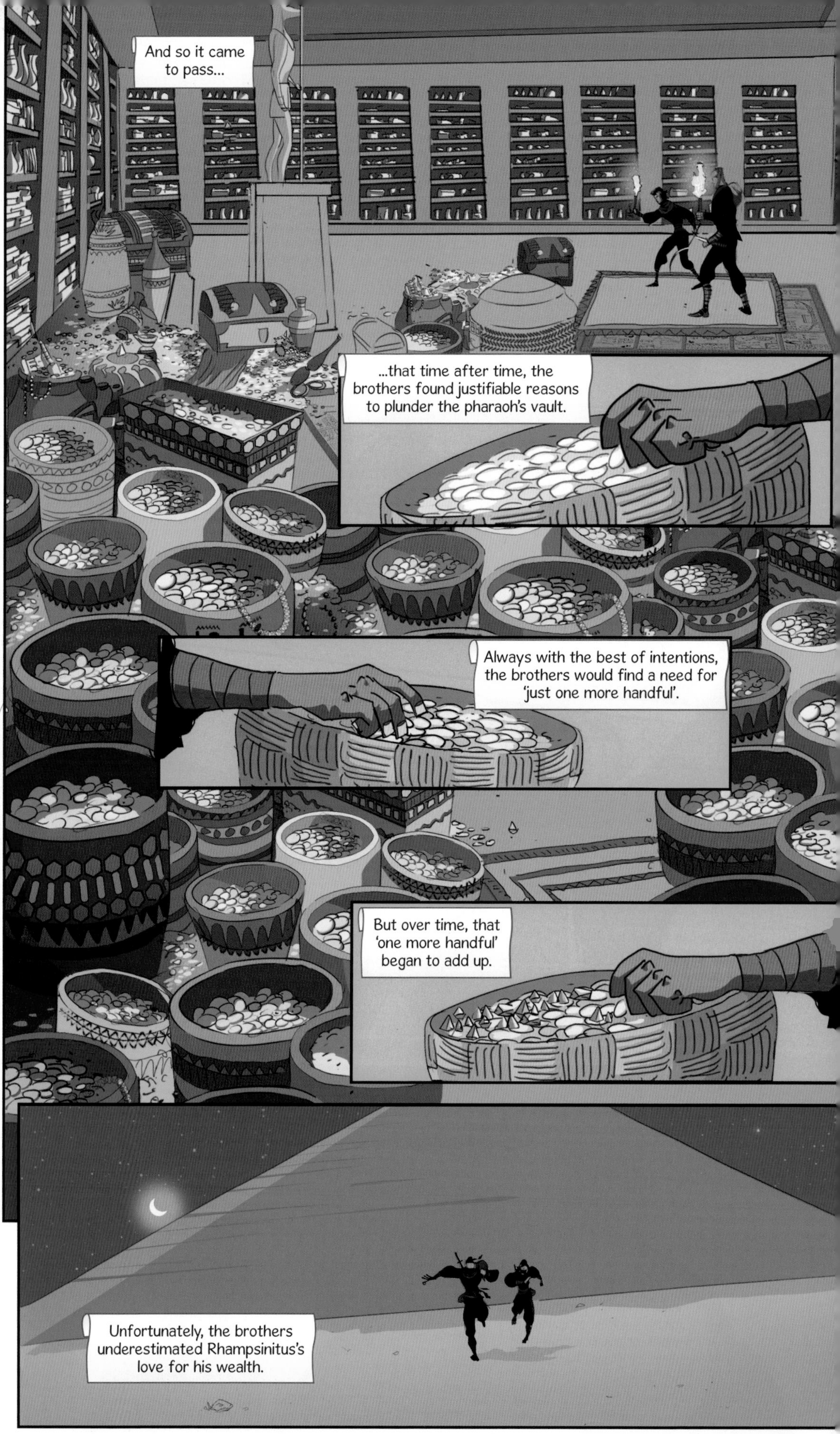
And so it came to pass...
...that time after time, the brothers found justifiable reasons to plunder the pharaoh's vault.
Always with the best of intentions, the brothers would find a need for 'just one more handful'.
But over time, that 'one more handful' began to add up.
Unfortunately, the brothers underestimated Rhampsinitus's love for his wealth.

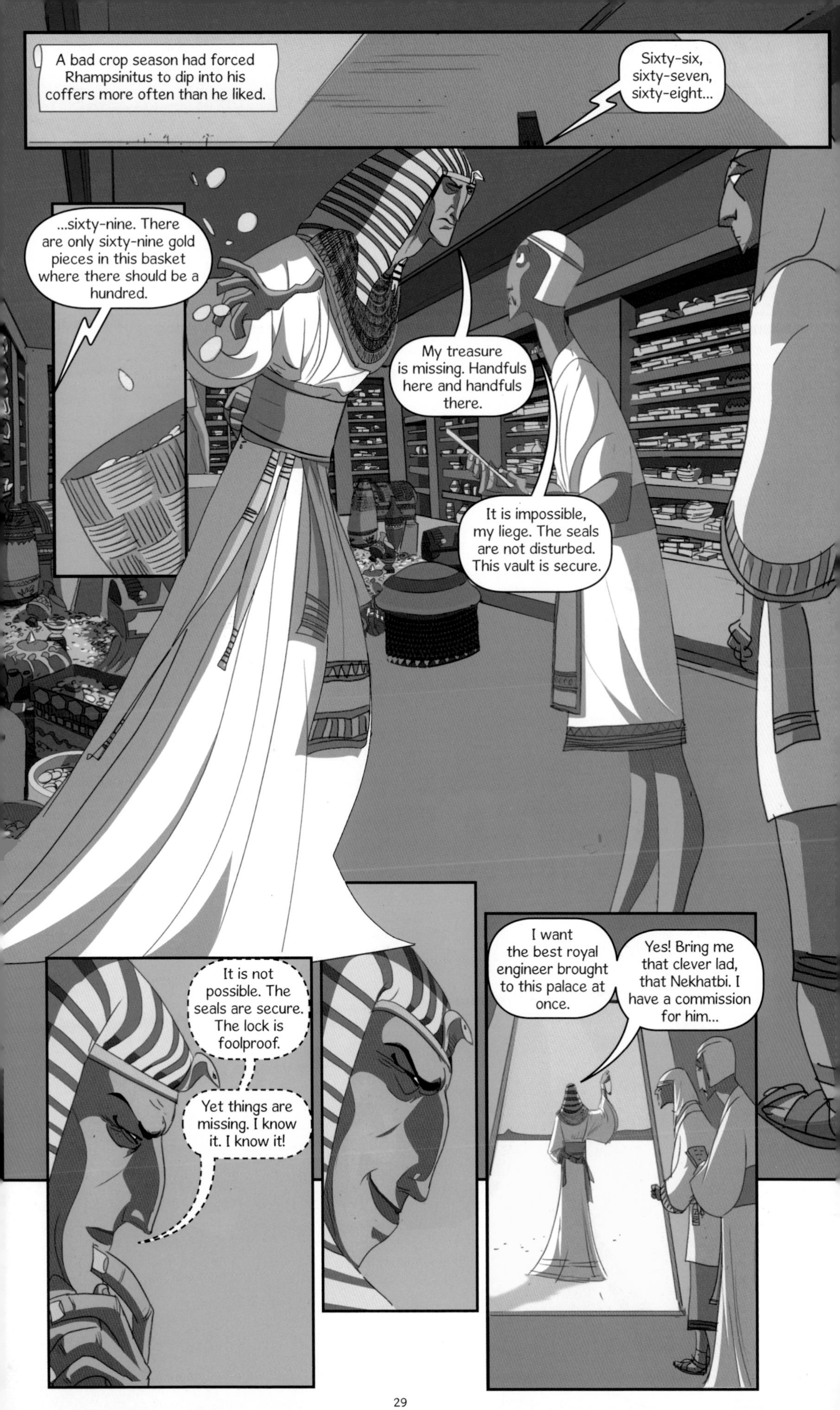

A bad crop season had forced Rhampsinitus to dip into his coffers more often than he liked.
Sixty-six, sixty-seven, sixty-eight...
...sixty-nine. There are only sixty-nine gold pieces in this basket where there should be a hundred.
My treasure is missing. Handfuls here and handfuls there.
It is impossible, my liege. The seals are not disturbed. This vault is secure.
It is not possible. The seals are secure. The lock is foolproof.
Yet things are missing. I know it. I know it!
I want the best royal engineer brought to this palace at once.
Yes! Bring me that clever lad, that Nekhatbi. I have a commission for him...

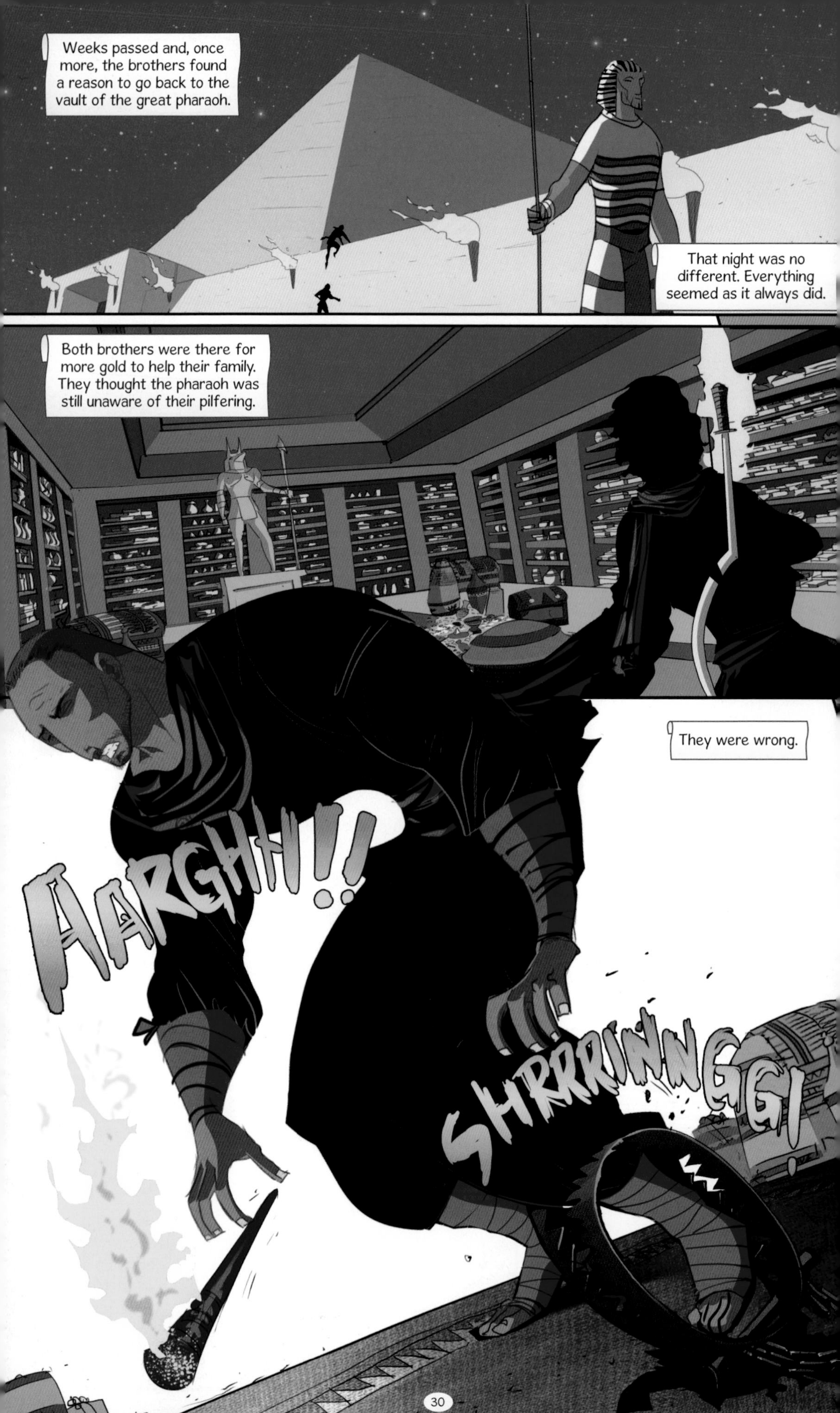
Weeks passed and, once more, the brothers found a reason to go back to the vault of the great pharaoh.
That night was no different. Everything seemed as it always did.
Both brothers were there for more gold to help their family. They thought the pharaoh was still unaware of their pilfering.
They were wrong.
AARGHH!!
SHRRRINNGG!

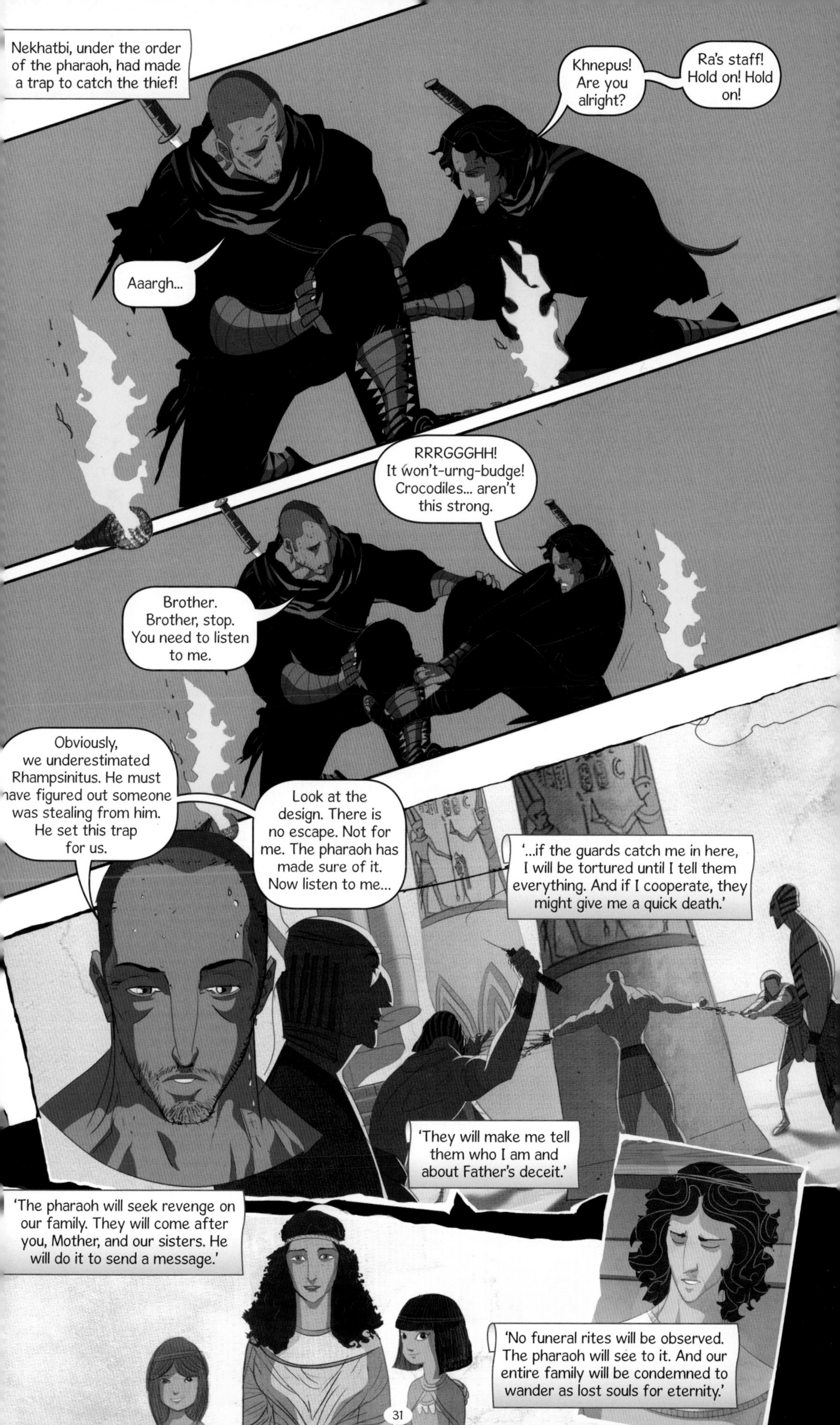
Nekhatbi, under the order of the pharaoh, had made a trap to catch the thief!
Khnepus! Are you alright?
Ra's staff! Hold on! Hold on!
Aaargh...
RRRGGGHH! It won't-urng-budge! Crocodiles... aren't this strong.
Brother. Brother, stop. You need to listen to me.
Obviously, we underestimated Rhampsinitus. He must have figured out someone was stealing from him. He set this trap for us.
Look at the design. There is no escape. Not for me. The pharaoh has made sure of it. Now listen to me...
'...if the guards catch me in here, I will be tortured until I tell them everything. And if I cooperate, they might give me a quick death.'
'They will make me tell them who I am and about Father's deceit.'
'The pharaoh will seek revenge on our family. They will come after you, Mother, and our sisters. He will do it to send a message.'
'No funeral rites will be observed. The pharaoh will see to it. And our entire family will be condemned to wander as lost souls for eternity.'

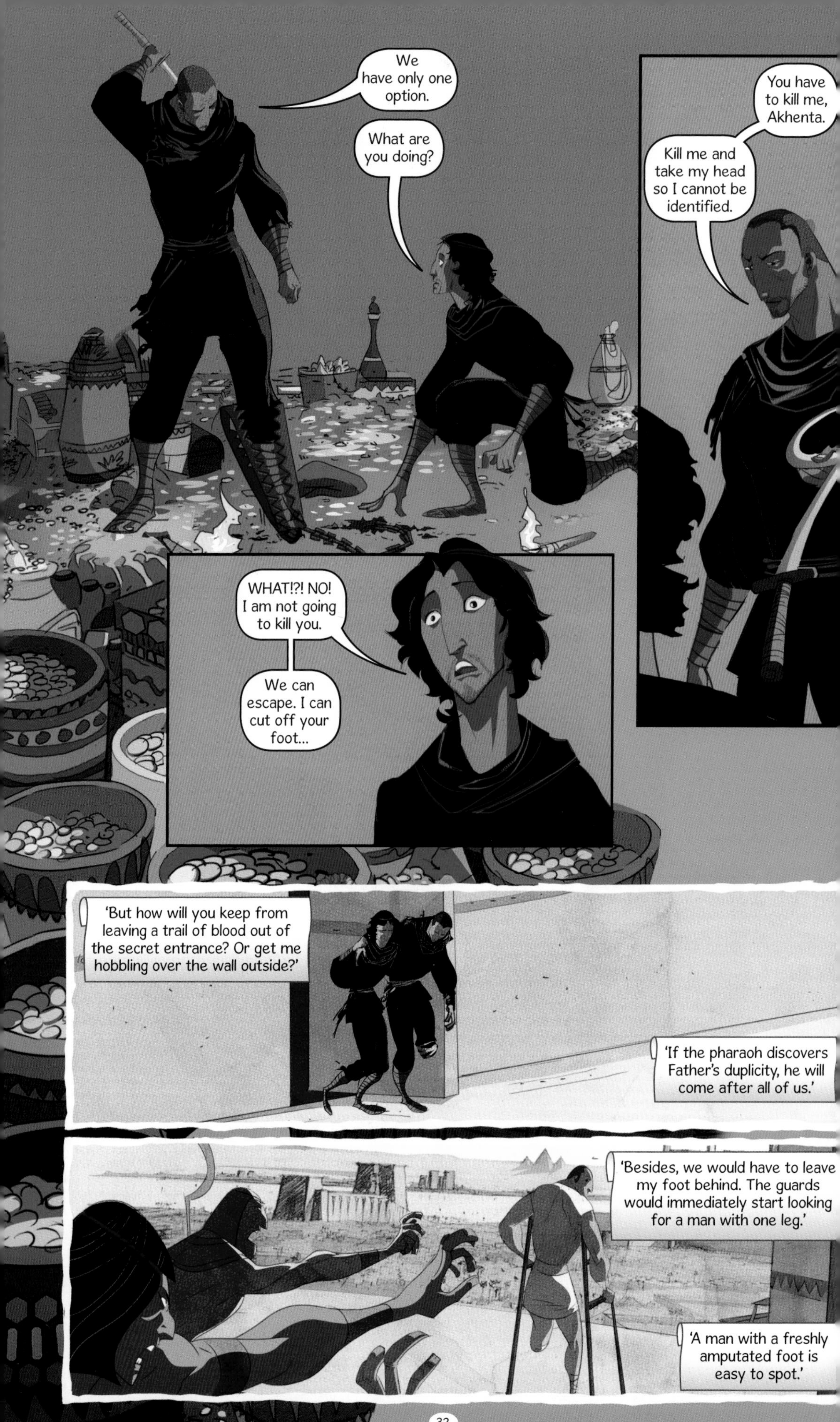
We have only one option.
What are you doing?
You have to kill me, Akhenta.
Kill me and take my head so I cannot be identified.
WHAT!?! NO! I am not going to kill you.
We can escape. I can cut off your foot...
'But how will you keep from leaving a trail of blood out of the secret entrance? Or get me hobbling over the wall outside?'
'If the pharaoh discovers Father's duplicity, he will come after all of us.'
'Besides, we would have to leave my foot behind. The guards would immediately start looking for a man with one leg.'
'A man with a freshly amputated foot is easy to spot.'

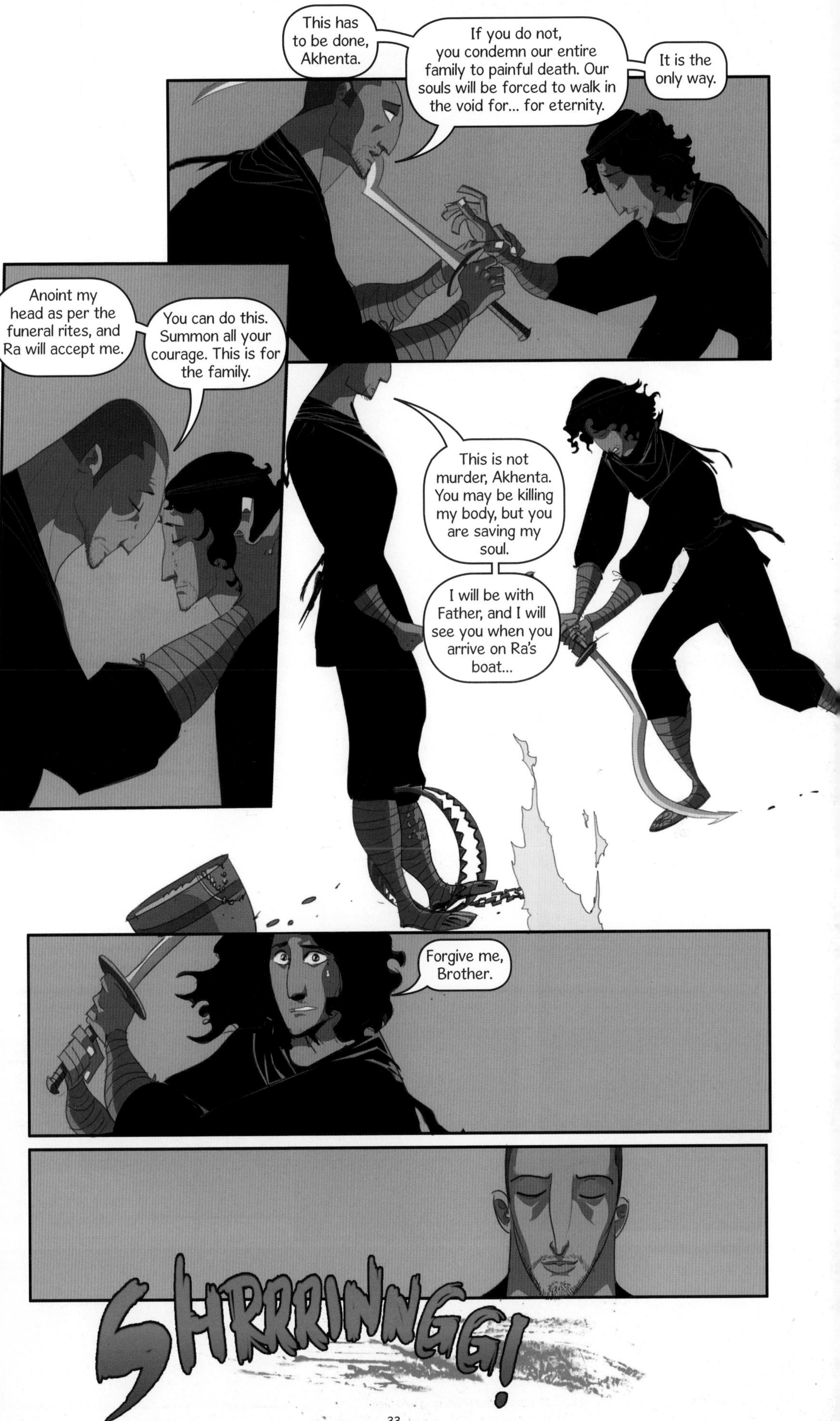
This has to be done, Akhenta.
If you do not, you condemn our entire family to painful death. Our souls will be forced to walk in the void for... for eternity.
It is the only way.
Anoint my head as per the funeral rites, and Ra will accept me.
You can do this. Summon all your courage. This is for the family.
This is not murder, Akhenta. You may be killing my body, but you are saving my soul.
I will be with Father, and I will see you when you arrive on Ra's boat...
Forgive me, Brother.
SHRRRINNGG!

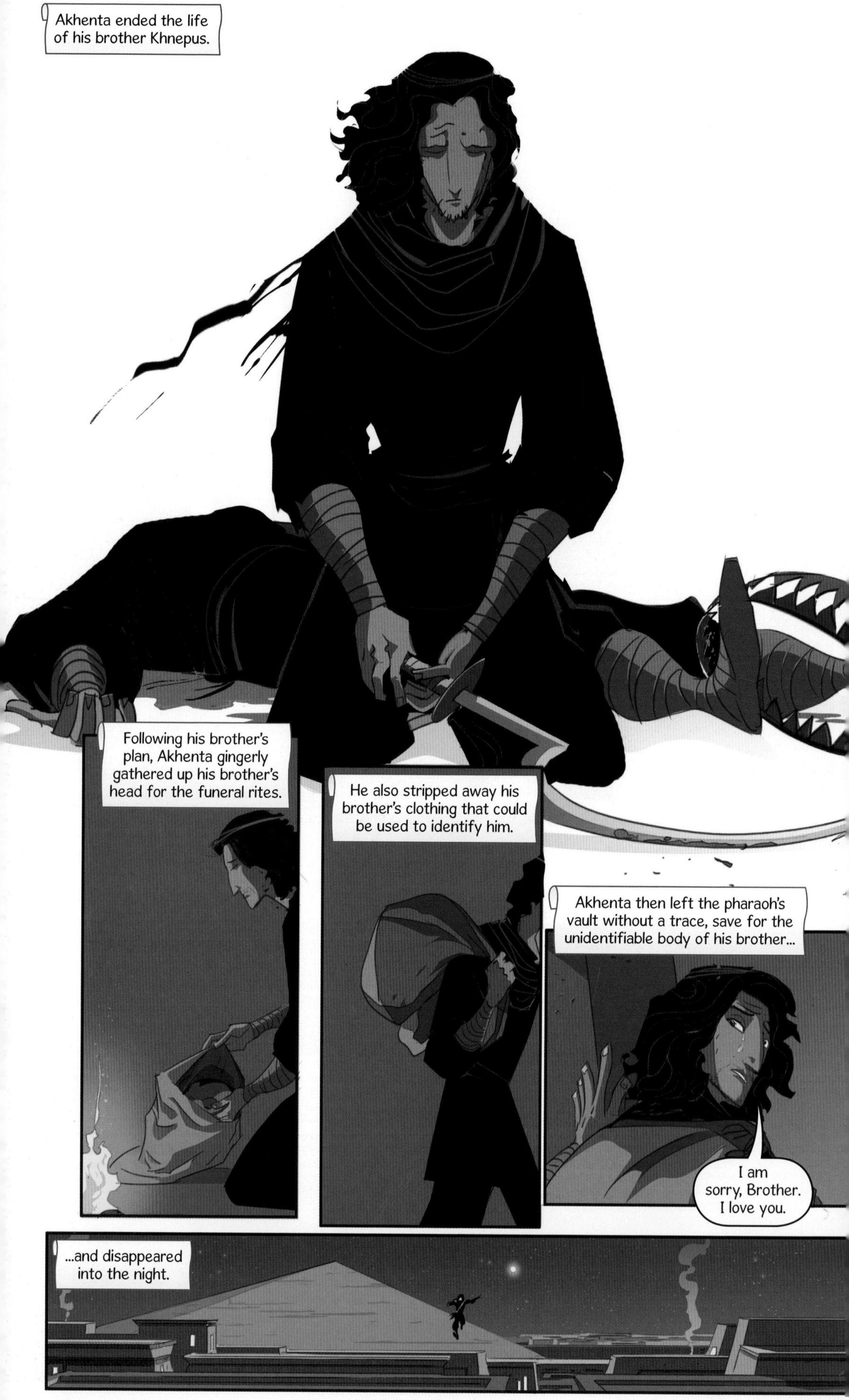

Akhenta ended the life of his brother Khnepus.
Following his brother's plan, Akhenta gingerly gathered up his brother's head for the funeral rites.
He also stripped away his brother's clothing that could be used to identify him.
Akhenta then left the pharaoh's vault without a trace, save for the unidentifiable body of his brother...
I am sorry, Brother. I love you.
...and disappeared into the night.

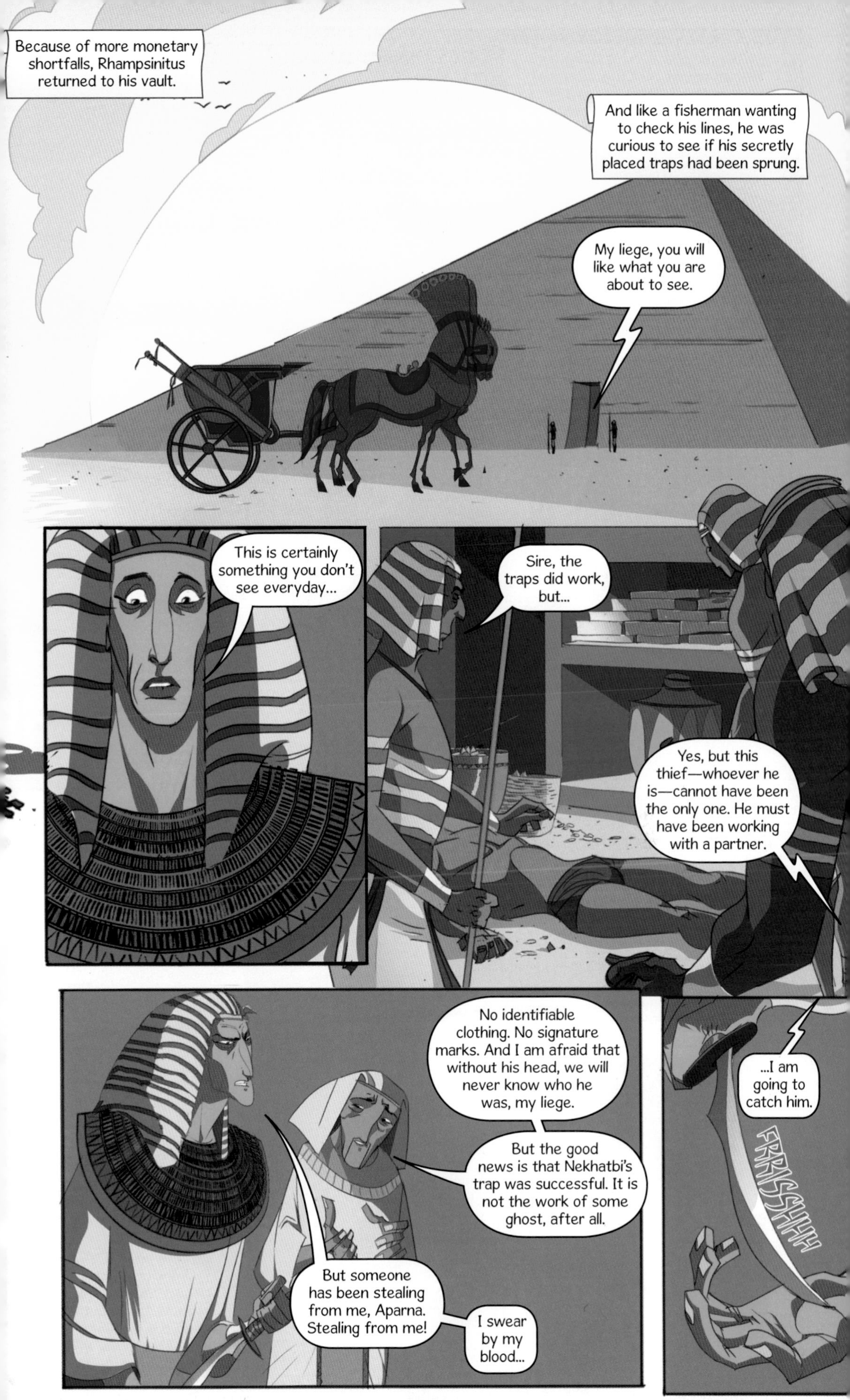

Because of more monetary shortfalls, Rhampsinitus returned to his vault.
And like a fisherman wanting to check his lines, he was curious to see if his secretly placed traps had been sprung.
My liege, you will like what you are about to see.
This is certainly something you don't see everyday...
Sire, the traps did work, but...
Yes, but this thief—whoever he is—cannot have been the only one. He must have been working with a partner.
No identifiable clothing. No signature marks. And I am afraid that without his head, we will never know who he was, my liege.
But the good news is that Nekhatbi's trap was successful. It is not the work of some ghost, after all.
But someone has been stealing from me, Aparna. Stealing from me!
I swear by my blood...
...I am going to catch him.
FRRISSHHH

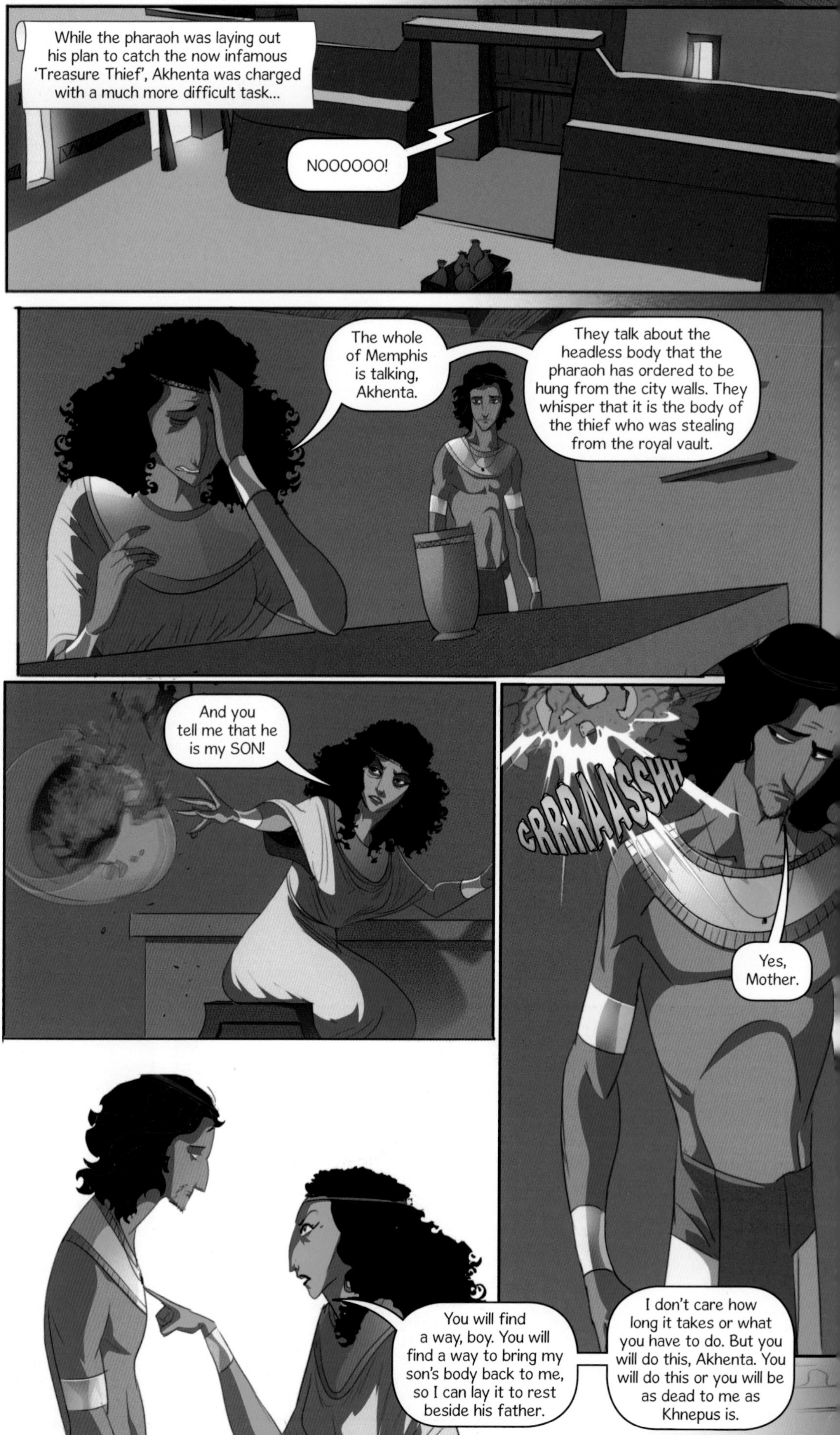
While the pharaoh was laying out his plan to catch the now infamous 'Treasure Thief', Akhenta was charged with a much more difficult task...
NOOOOOO!
The whole of Memphis is talking, Akhenta.
They talk about the headless body that the pharaoh has ordered to be hung from the city walls. They whisper that it is the body of the thief who was stealing from the royal vault.
And you tell me that he is my SON!
CRRRAASSHH
Yes, Mother.
You will find a way, boy. You will find a way to bring my son's body back to me, so I can lay it to rest beside his father.
I don't care how long it takes or what you have to do. But you will do this, Akhenta. You will do this or you will be as dead to me as Khnepus is.

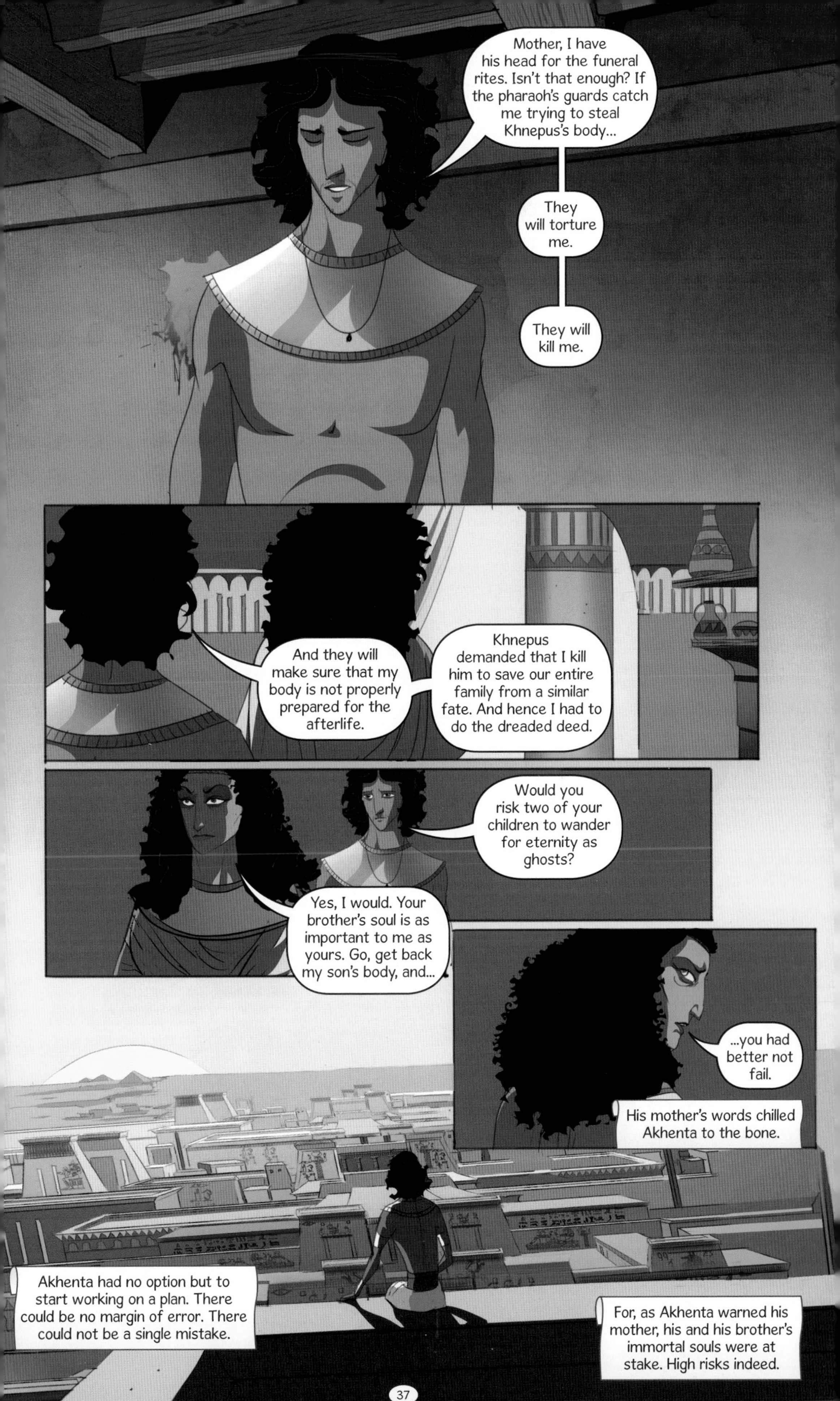
Mother, I have his head for the funeral rites. Isn't that enough? If the pharaoh's guards catch me trying to steal Khnepus's body...
They will torture me.
They will kill me.
And they will make sure that my body is not properly prepared for the afterlife.
Khnepus demanded that I kill him to save our entire family from a similar fate. And hence I had to do the dreaded deed.
Would you risk two of your children to wander for eternity as ghosts?
Yes, I would. Your brother's soul is as important to me as yours. Go, get back my son's body, and...
...you had better not fail.
His mother's words chilled Akhenta to the bone.
Akhenta had no option but to start working on a plan. There could be no margin of error. There could not be a single mistake.
For, as Akhenta warned his mother, his and his brother's immortal souls were at stake. High risks indeed.

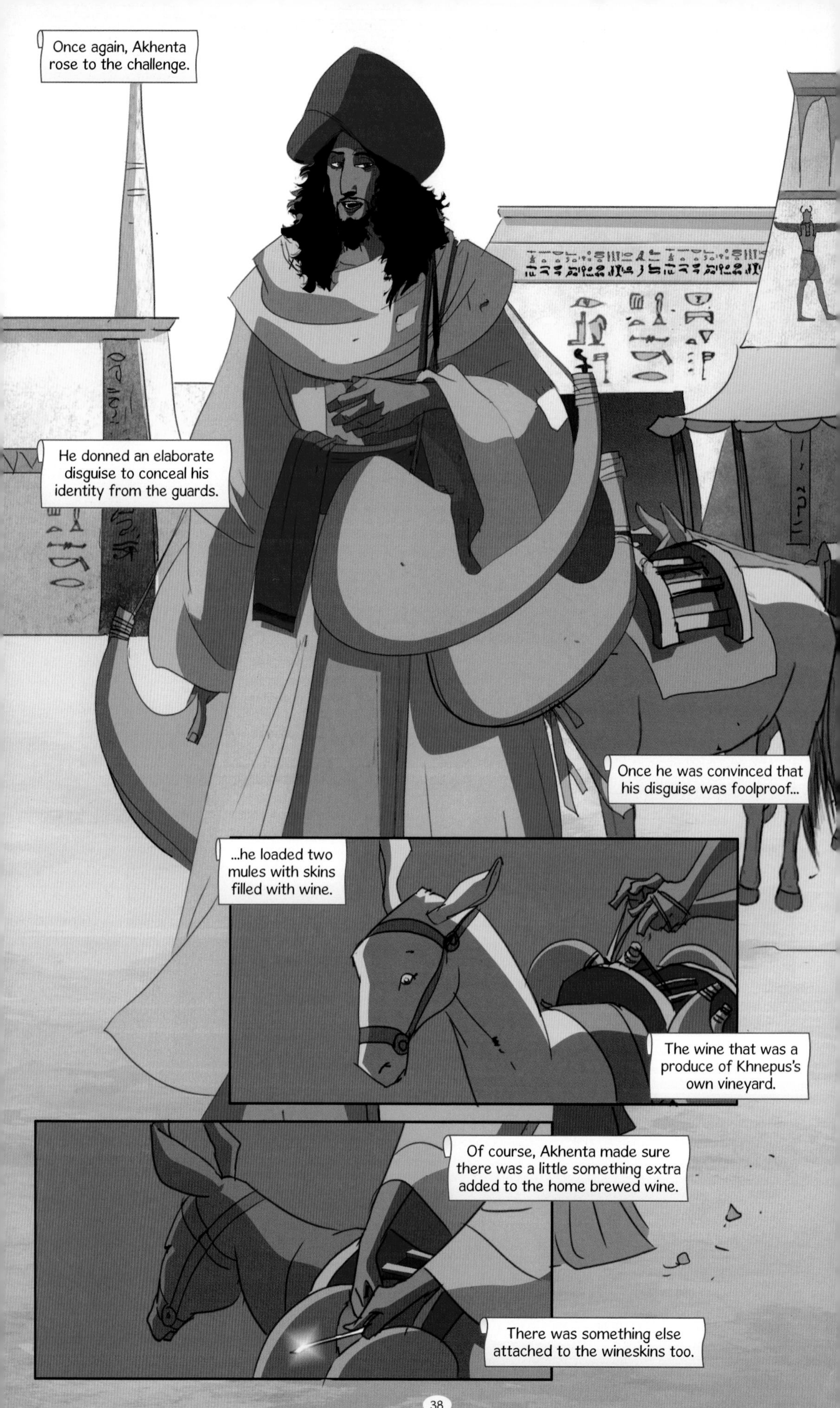
Once again, Akhenta rose to the challenge.
He donned an elaborate disguise to conceal his identity from the guards.
Once he was convinced that his disguise was foolproof...
...he loaded two mules with skins filled with wine.
The wine that was a produce of Khnepus's own vineyard.
Of course, Akhenta made sure there was a little something extra added to the home brewed wine.
There was something else attached to the wineskins too.

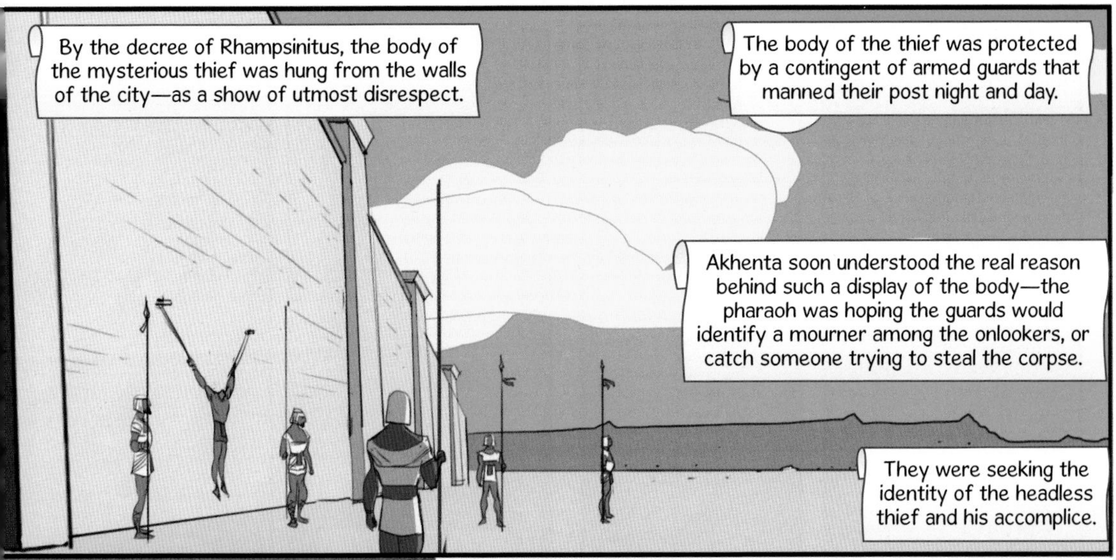
By the decree of Rhampsinitus, the body of the mysterious thief was hung from the walls of the city—as a show of utmost disrespect.
The body of the thief was protected by a contingent of armed guards that manned their post night and day.
Akhenta soon understood the real reason behind such a display of the body—the pharaoh was hoping the guards would identify a mourner among the onlookers, or catch someone trying to steal the corpse.
They were seeking the identity of the headless thief and his accomplice.

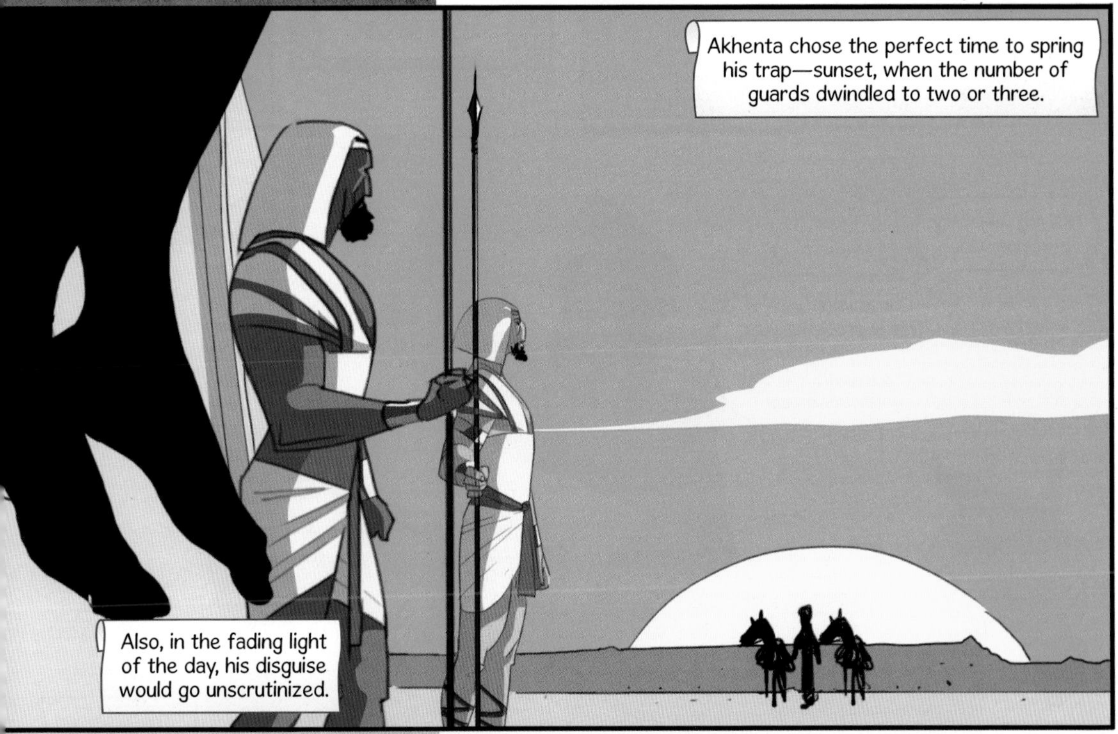
Akhenta chose the perfect time to spring his trap—sunset, when the number of guards dwindled to two or three.
Also, in the fading light of the day, his disguise would go unscrutinized.

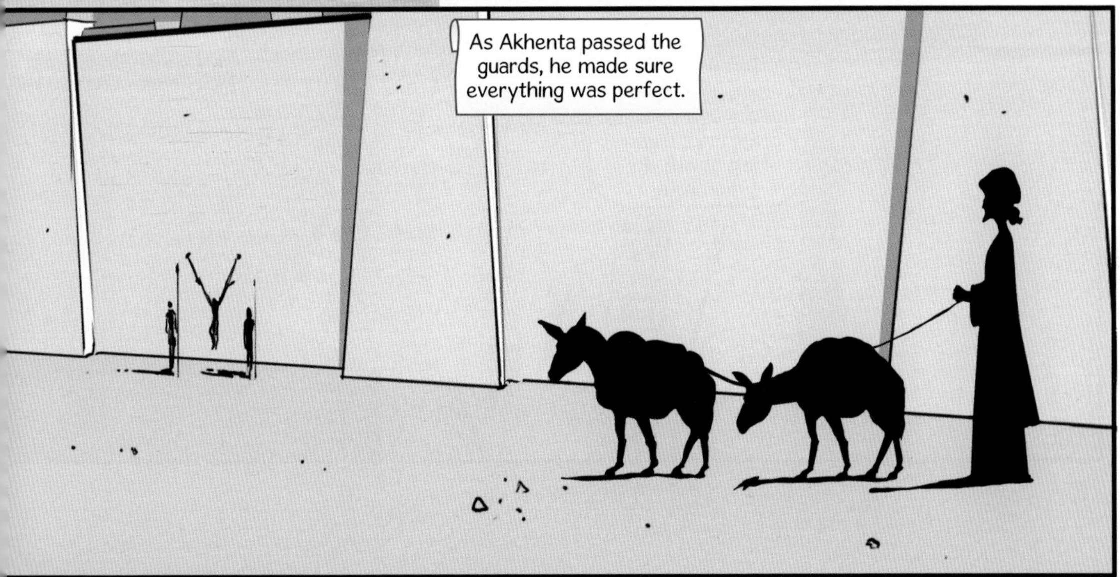
As Akhenta passed the guards, he made sure everything was perfect.

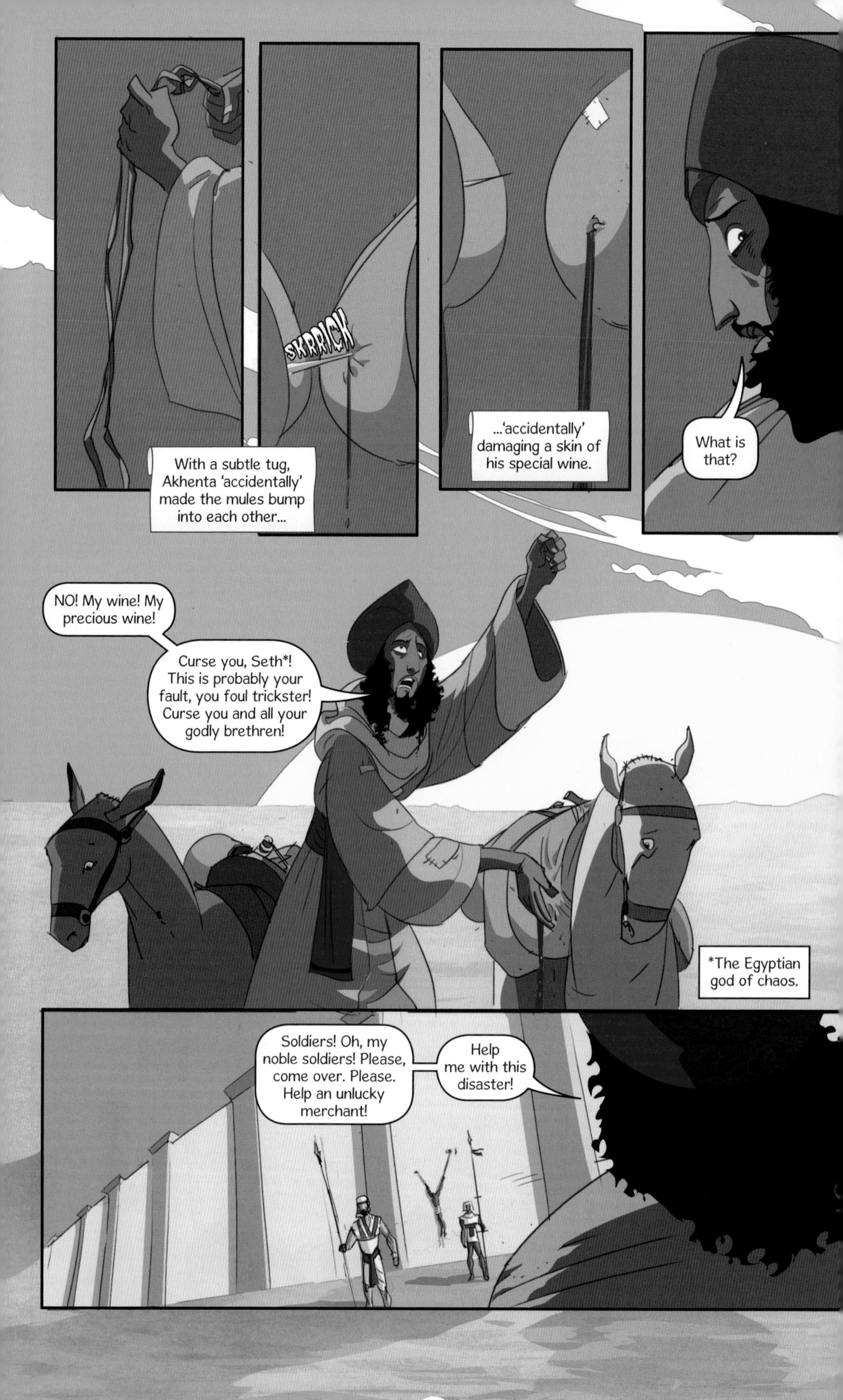
SKRRICH
With a subtle tug, Akhenta 'accidentally' made the mules bump into each other...
...'accidentally' damaging a skin of his special wine.
What is that?
NO! My wine! My precious wine!
Curse you, Seth*! This is probably your fault, you foul trickster! Curse you and all your godly brethren!
*The Egyptian god of chaos.
Soldiers! Oh, my noble soldiers! Please, come over. Please. Help an unlucky merchant!
Help me with this disaster!

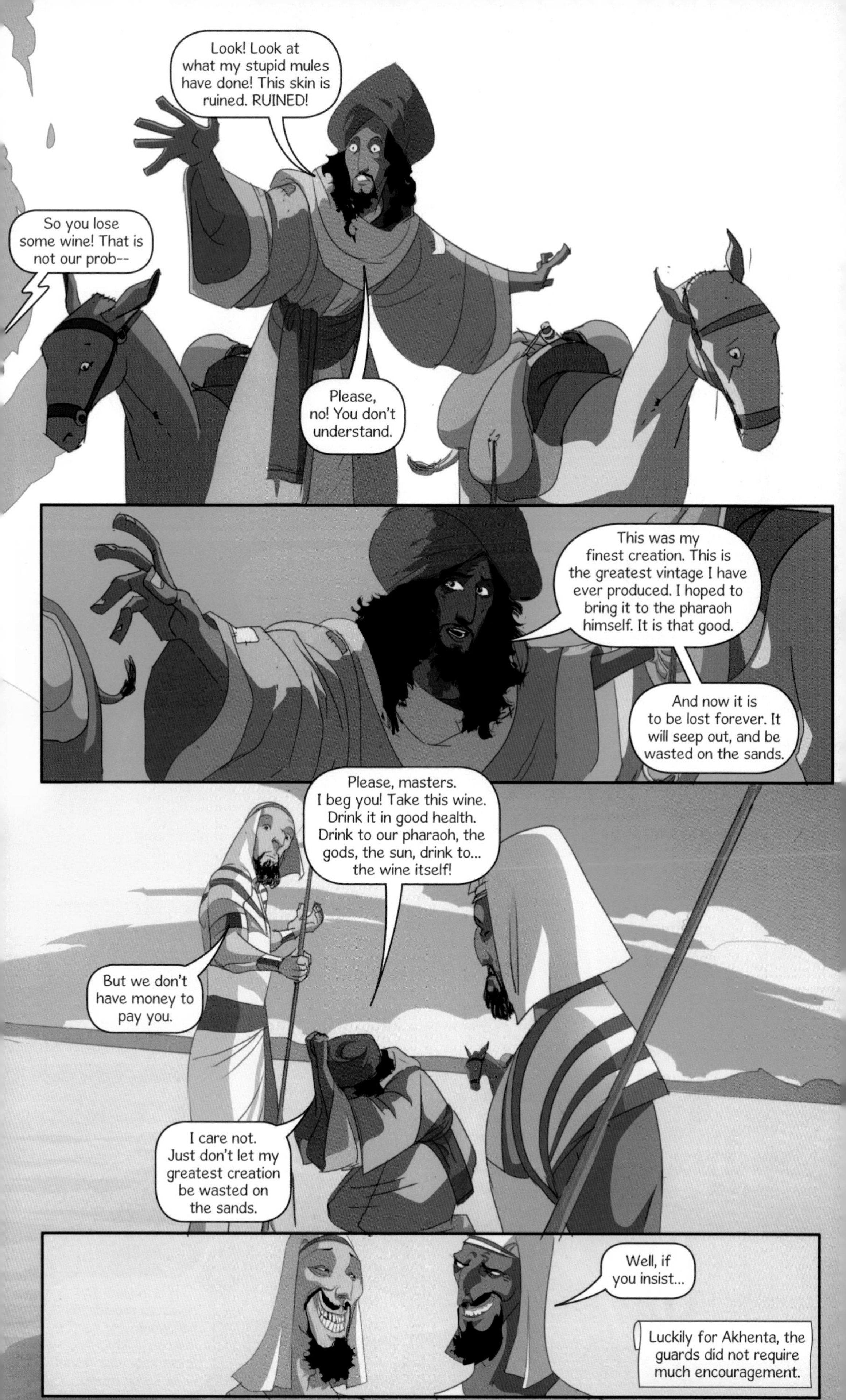
Look! Look at what my stupid mules have done! This skin is ruined. RUINED!
So you lose some wine! That is not our prob--
Please, no! You don't understand.
This was my finest creation. This is the greatest vintage I have ever produced. I hoped to bring it to the pharaoh himself. It is that good.
And now it is to be lost forever. It will seep out, and be wasted on the sands.
Please, masters. I beg you! Take this wine. Drink it in good health. Drink to our pharaoh, the gods, the sun, drink to... the wine itself!
But we don't have money to pay you.
I care not. Just don't let my greatest creation be wasted on the sands.
Well, if you insist...
Luckily for Akhenta, the guards did not require much encouragement.

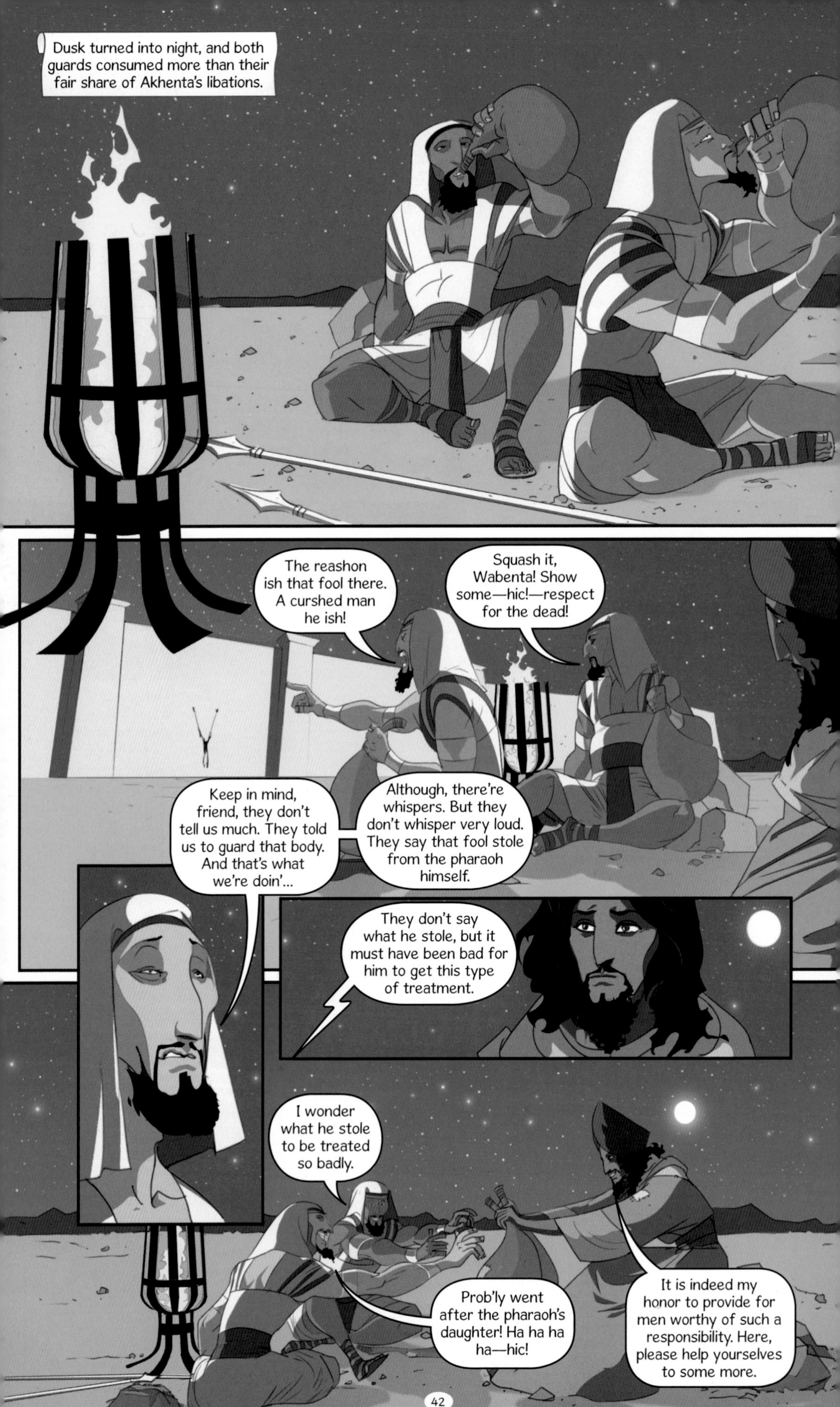
Dusk turned into night, and both guards consumed more than their fair share of Akhenta's libations.
The reashon ish that fool there. A curshed man he ish!
Squash it, Wabenta! Show some—hic!—respect for the dead!
Although, there're whispers. But they don't whisper very loud. They say that fool stole from the pharaoh himself.
Keep in mind, friend, they don't tell us much. They told us to guard that body. And that's what we're doin'...
They don't say what he stole, but it must have been bad for him to get this type of treatment.
I wonder what he stole to be treated so badly.
Prob'ly went after the pharaoh's daughter! Ha ha ha ha—hic!
It is indeed my honor to provide for men worthy of such a responsibility. Here, please help yourselves to some more.

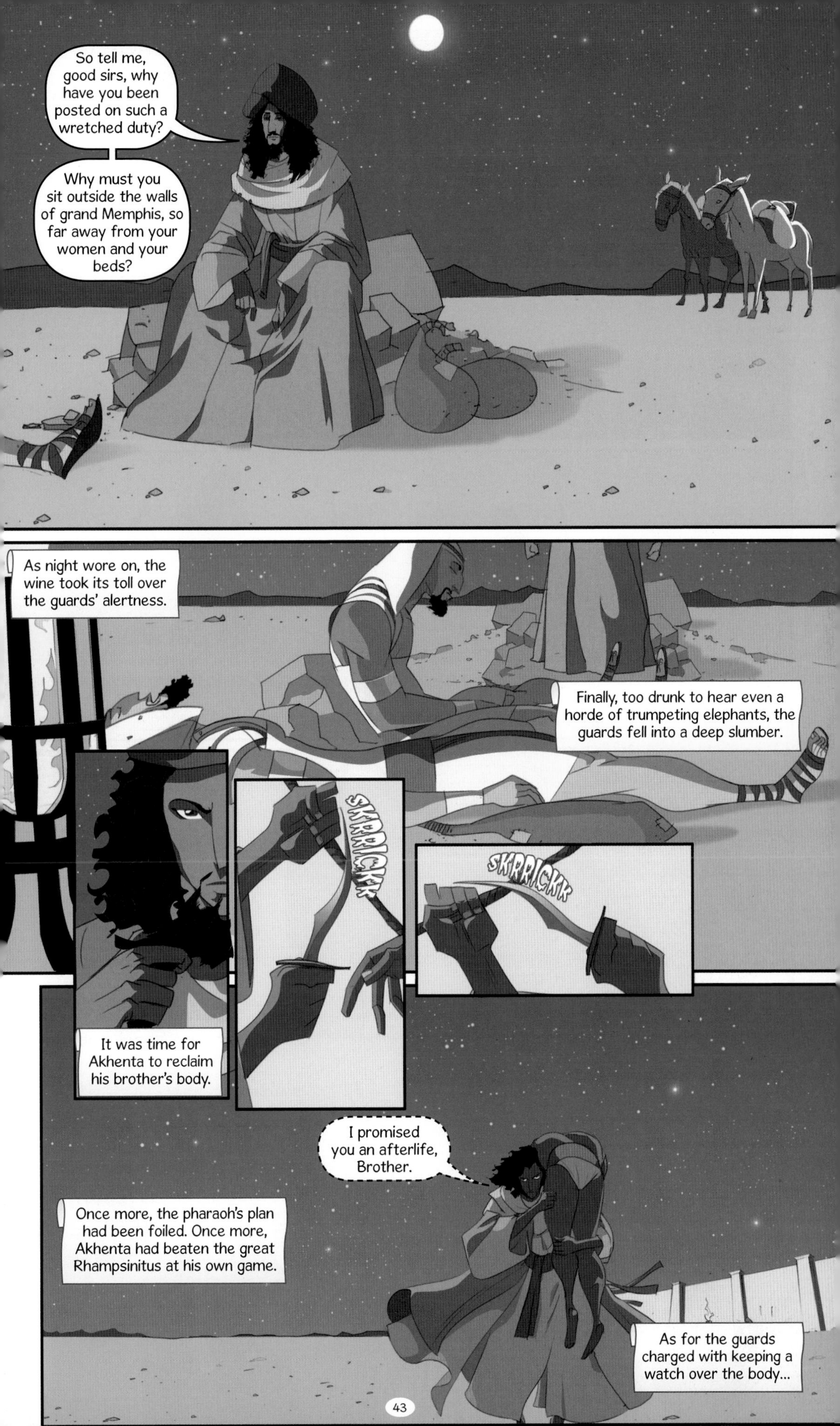

So tell me, good sirs, why have you been posted on such a wretched duty?
Why must you sit outside the walls of grand Memphis, so far away from your women and your beds?
As night wore on, the wine took its toll over the guards' alertness.
Finally, too drunk to hear even a horde of trumpeting elephants, the guards fell into a deep slumber.
It was time for Akhenta to reclaim his brother's body.
SKRRICKK
SKRRICKK
I promised you an afterlife, Brother.
Once more, the pharaoh's plan had been foiled. Once more, Akhenta had beaten the great Rhampsinitus at his own game.
As for the guards charged with keeping a watch over the body...

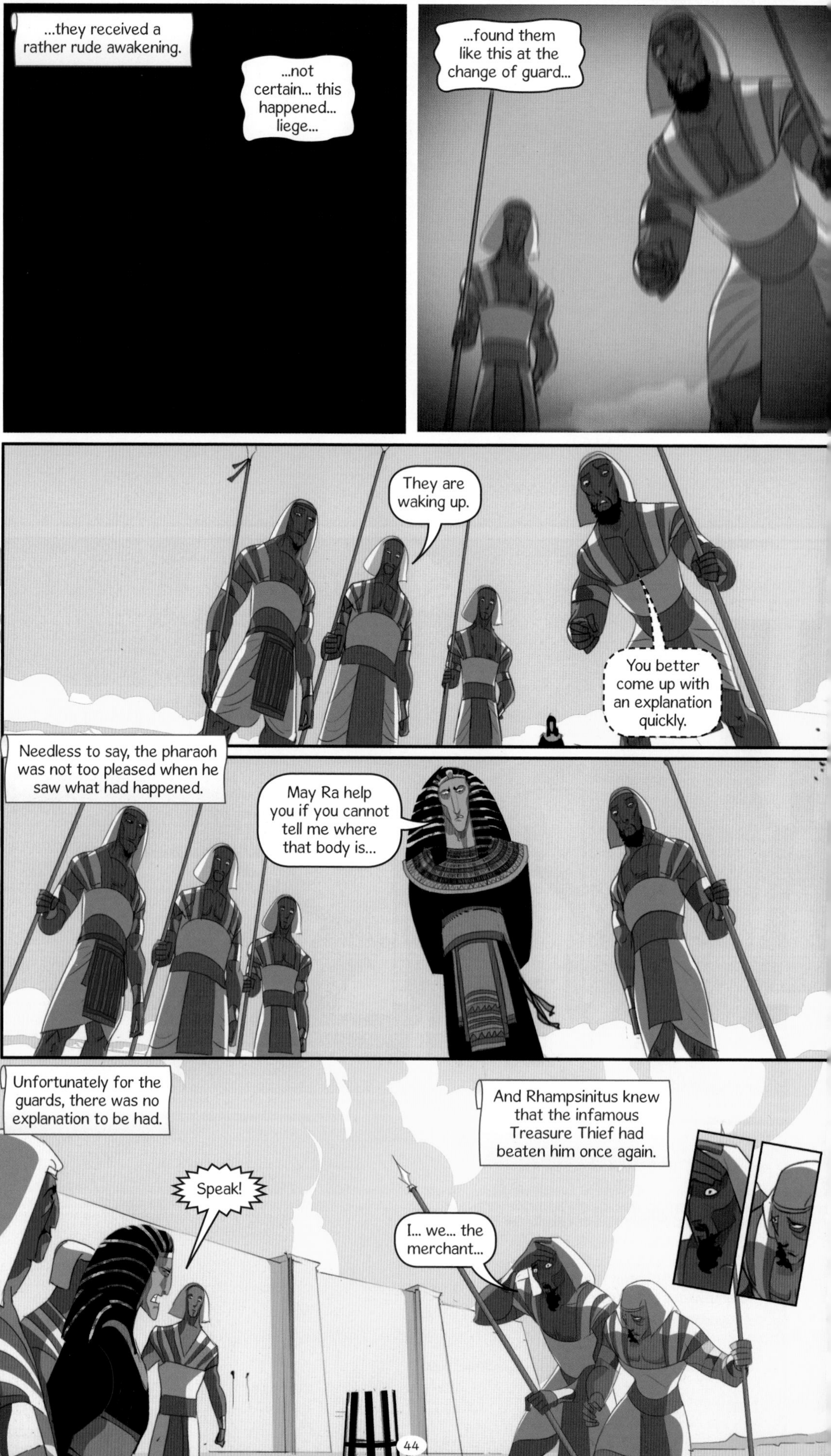
...they received a rather rude awakening.
...not certain... this happened... liege...
...found them like this at the change of guard...
They are waking up.
You better come up with an explanation quickly.
Needless to say, the pharaoh was not too pleased when he saw what had happened.
May Ra help you if you cannot tell me where that body is...
Unfortunately for the guards, there was no explanation to be had.
Speak!
And Rhampsinitus knew that the infamous Treasure Thief had beaten him once again.
I... we... the merchant...

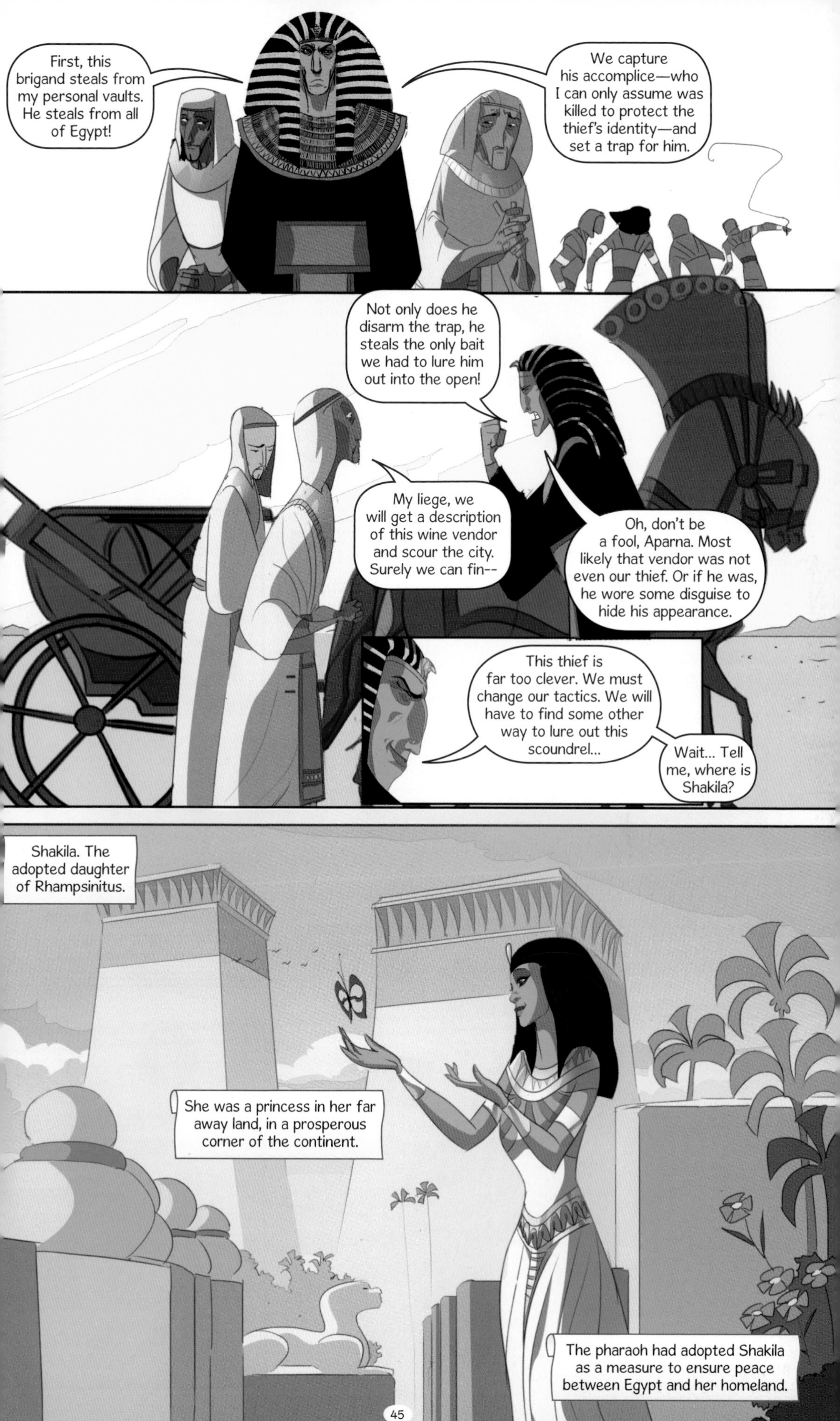

First, this brigand steals from my personal vaults. He steals from all of Egypt!
We capture his accomplice—who I can only assume was killed to protect the thief's identity—and set a trap for him.
Not only does he disarm the trap, he steals the only bait we had to lure him out into the open!
My liege, we will get a description of this wine vendor and scour the city. Surely we can fin--
Oh, don't be a fool, Aparna. Most likely that vendor was not even our thief. Or if he was, he wore some disguise to hide his appearance.
This thief is far too clever. We must change our tactics. We will have to find some other way to lure out this scoundrel...
Wait... Tell me, where is Shakila?
Shakila. The adopted daughter of Rhampsinitus.
She was a princess in her far away land, in a prosperous corner of the continent.
The pharaoh had adopted Shakila as a measure to ensure peace between Egypt and her homeland.

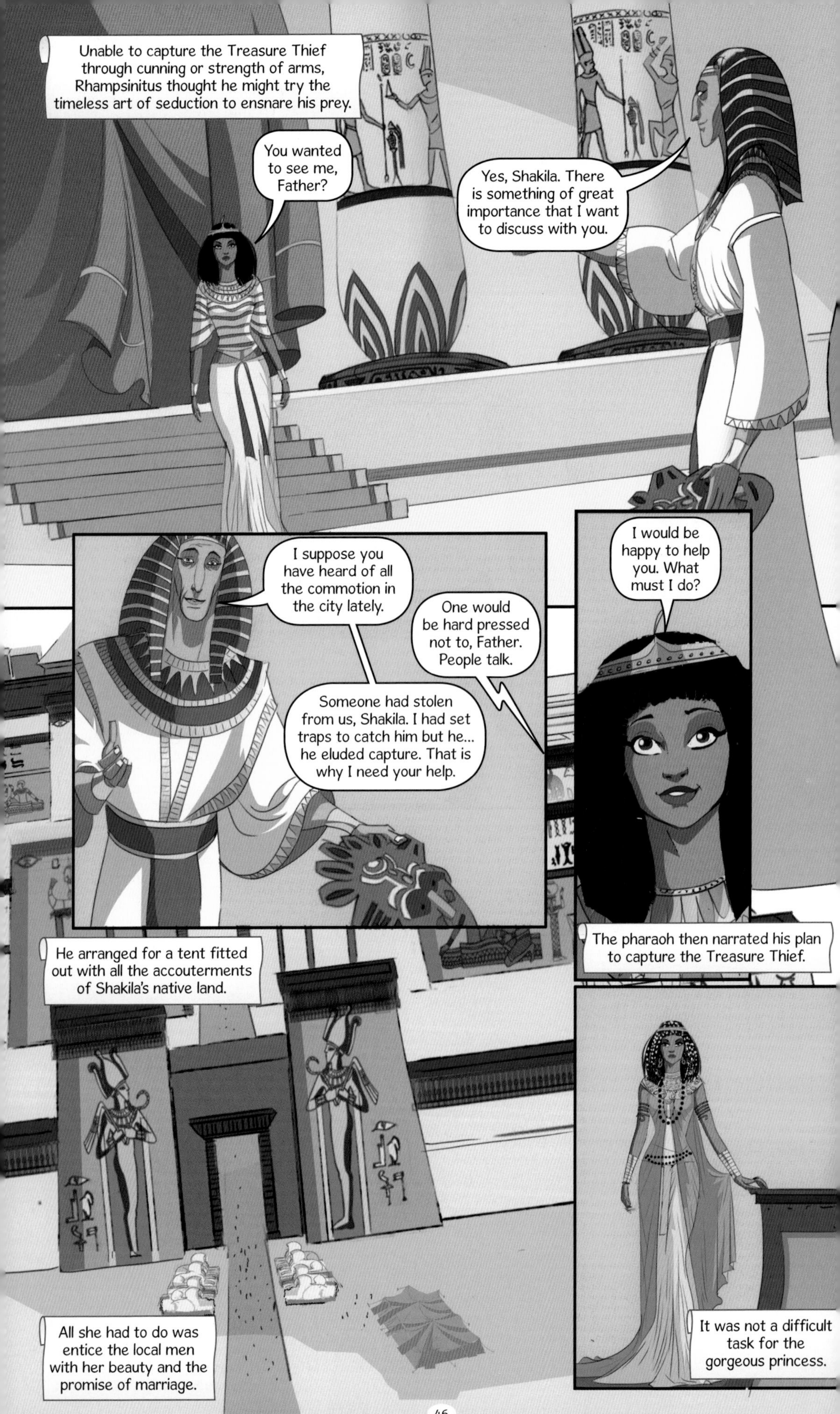
Unable to capture the Treasure Thief through cunning or strength of arms, Rhampsinitus thought he might try the timeless art of seduction to ensnare his prey.
You wanted to see me, Father?
Yes, Shakila. There is something of great importance that I want to discuss with you.
I suppose you have heard of all the commotion in the city lately.
One would be hard pressed not to, Father. People talk.
Someone had stolen from us, Shakila. I had set traps to catch him but he... he eluded capture. That is why I need your help.
I would be happy to help you. What must I do?
The pharaoh then narrated his plan to capture the Treasure Thief.
He arranged for a tent fitted out with all the accouterments of Shakila's native land.
All she had to do was entice the local men with her beauty and the promise of marriage.
It was not a difficult task for the gorgeous princess.

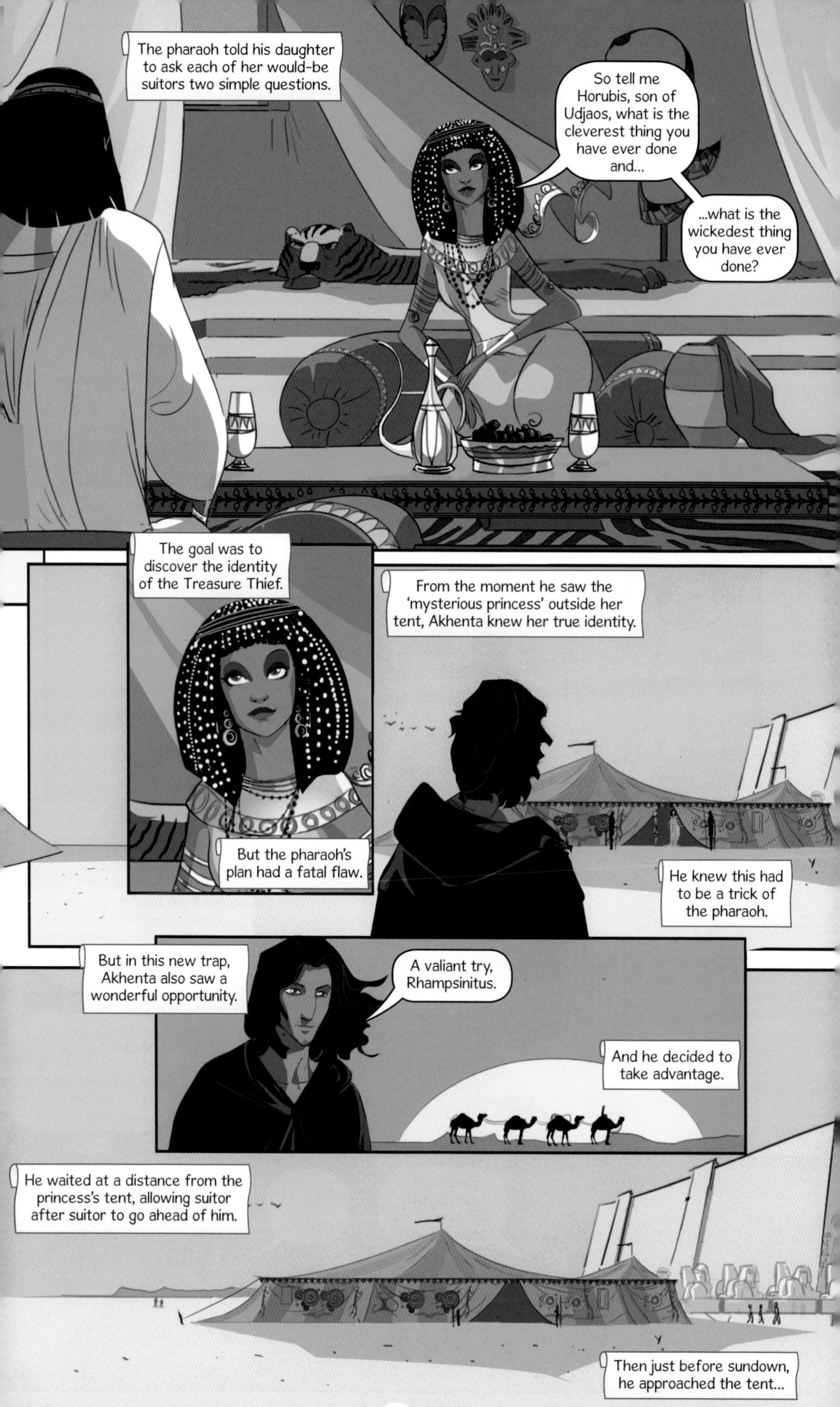
The pharaoh told his daughter to ask each of her would-be suitors two simple questions.
So tell me Horubis, son of Udjaos, what is the cleverest thing you have ever done and...
...what is the wickedest thing you have ever done?
The goal was to discover the identity of the Treasure Thief.
But the pharaoh's plan had a fatal flaw.
From the moment he saw the 'mysterious princess' outside her tent, Akhenta knew her true identity.
He knew this had to be a trick of the pharaoh.
But in this new trap, Akhenta also saw a wonderful opportunity.
A valiant try, Rhampsinitus.
And he decided to take advantage.
He waited at a distance from the princess's tent, allowing suitor after suitor to go ahead of him.
Then just before sundown, he approached the tent...

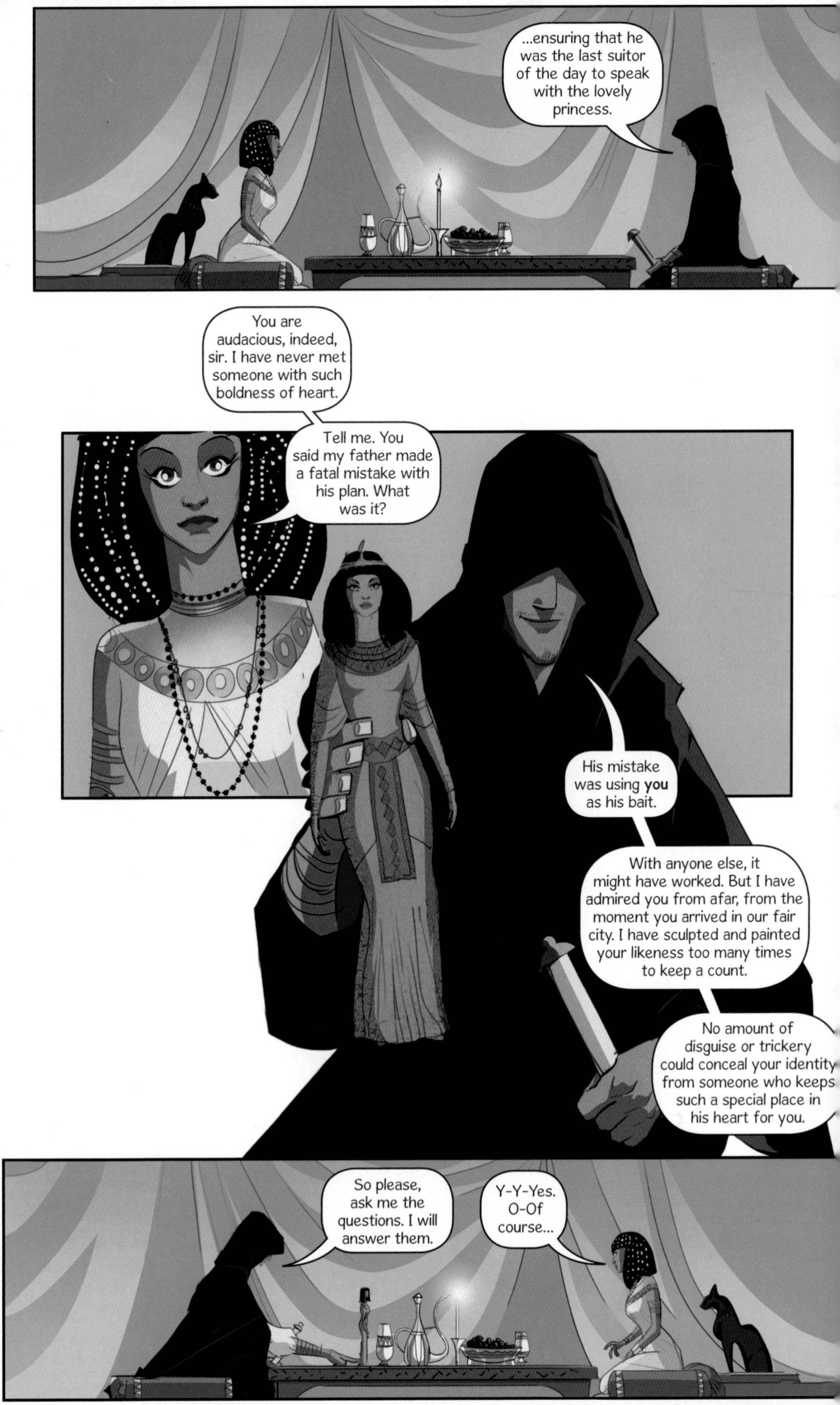
...ensuring that he was the last suitor of the day to speak with the lovely princess.
You are audacious, indeed, sir. I have never met someone with such boldness of heart.
Tell me. You said my father made a fatal mistake with his plan. What was it?
His mistake was using **you** as his bait.
With anyone else, it might have worked. But I have admired you from afar, from the moment you arrived in our fair city. I have sculpted and painted your likeness too many times to keep a count.
No amount of disguise or trickery could conceal your identity from someone who keeps such a special place in his heart for you.
So please, ask me the questions. I will answer them.
Y-Y-Yes. O-Of course...

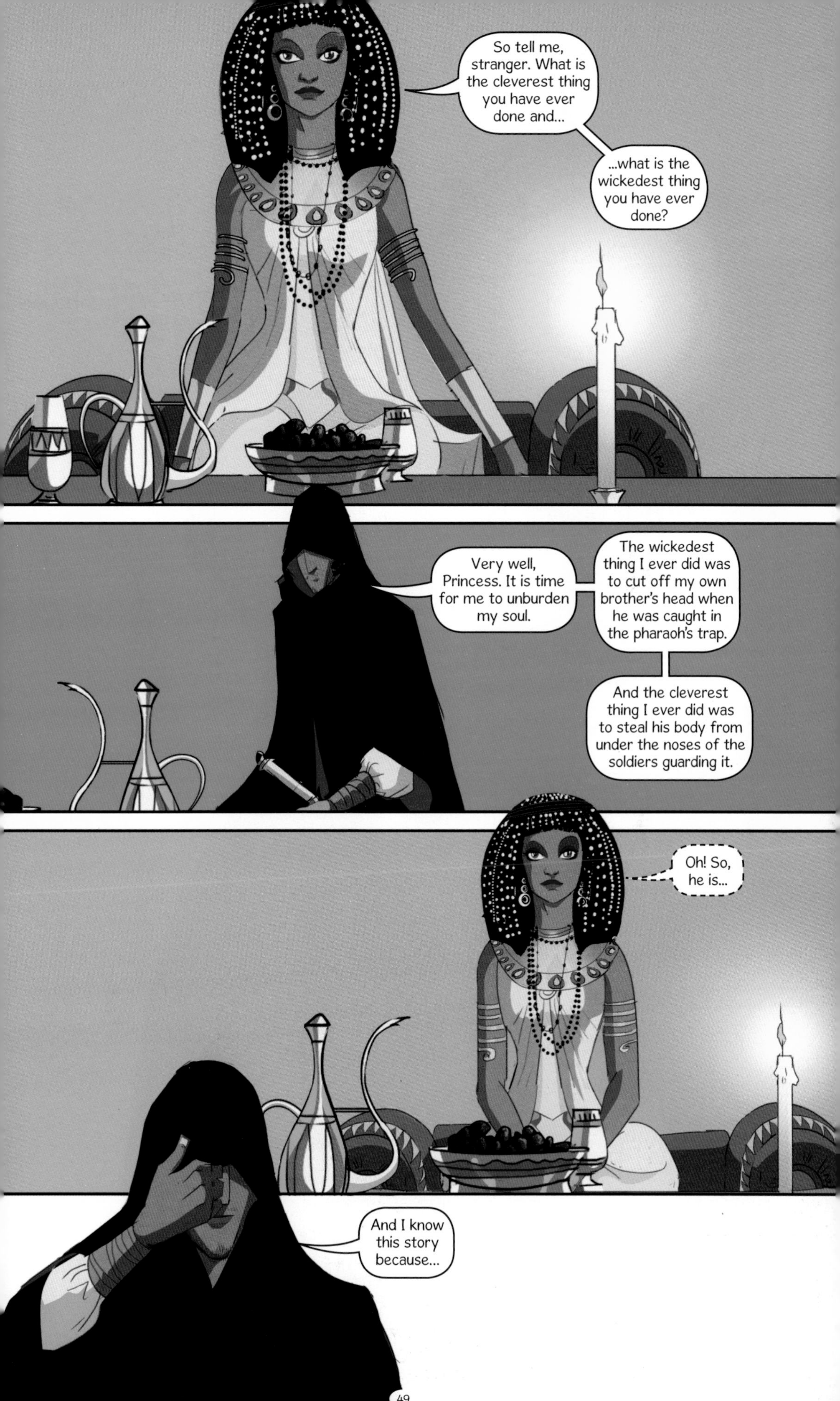
So tell me, stranger. What is the cleverest thing you have ever done and...
...what is the wickedest thing you have ever done?
Very well, Princess. It is time for me to unburden my soul.
The wickedest thing I ever did was to cut off my own brother's head when he was caught in the pharaoh's trap.
And the cleverest thing I ever did was to steal his body from under the noses of the soldiers guarding it.
Oh! So, he is...
And I know this story because...

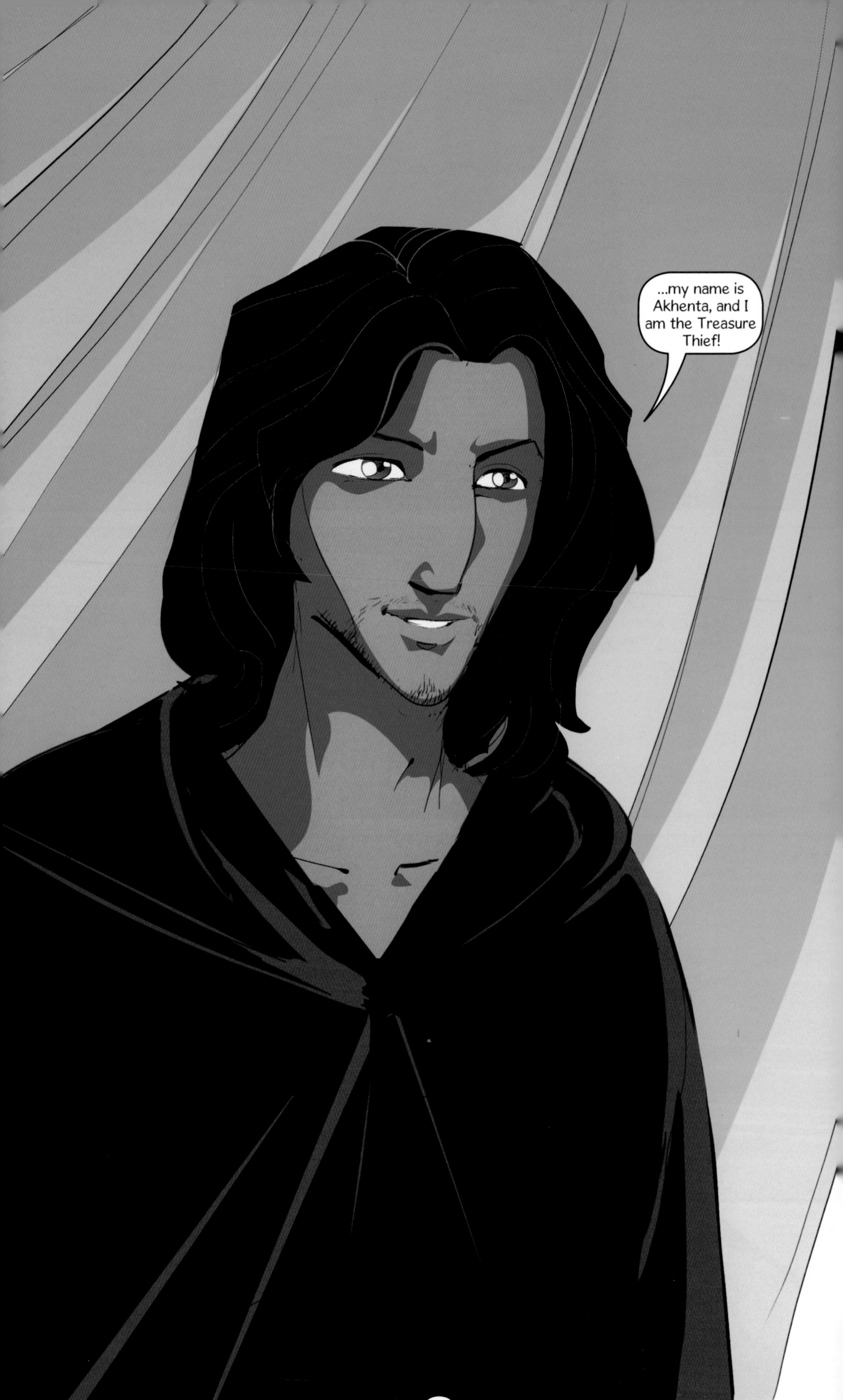
...my name is Akhenta, and I am the Treasure Thief!

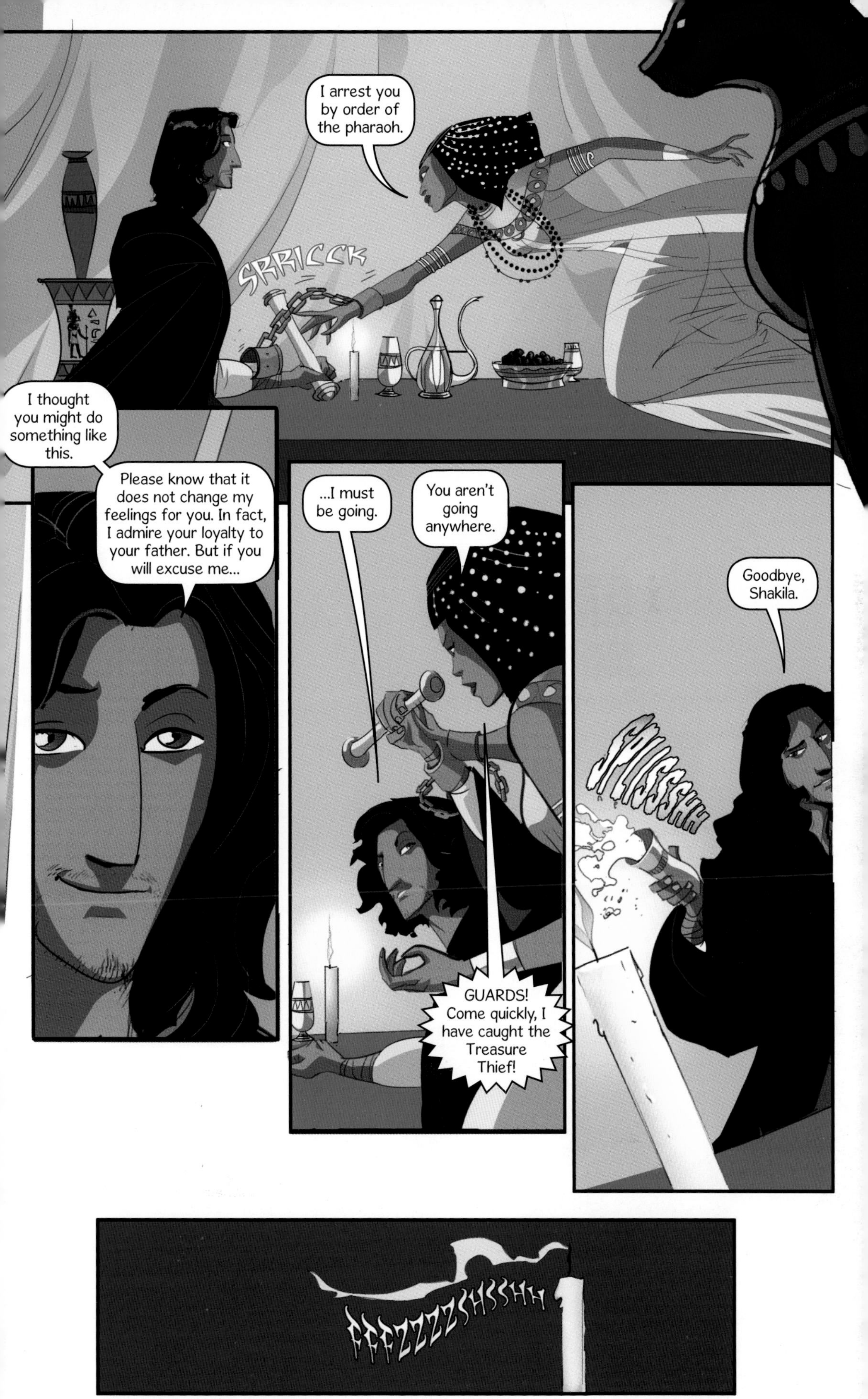
I arrest you by order of the pharaoh.
SRRICCK
I thought you might do something like this.
Please know that it does not change my feelings for you. In fact, I admire your loyalty to your father. But if you will excuse me...
...I must be going.
You aren't going anywhere.
GUARDS! Come quickly, I have caught the Treasure Thief!
Goodbye, Shakila.
SPLISSSHH
FFFZZZZSHSSHH

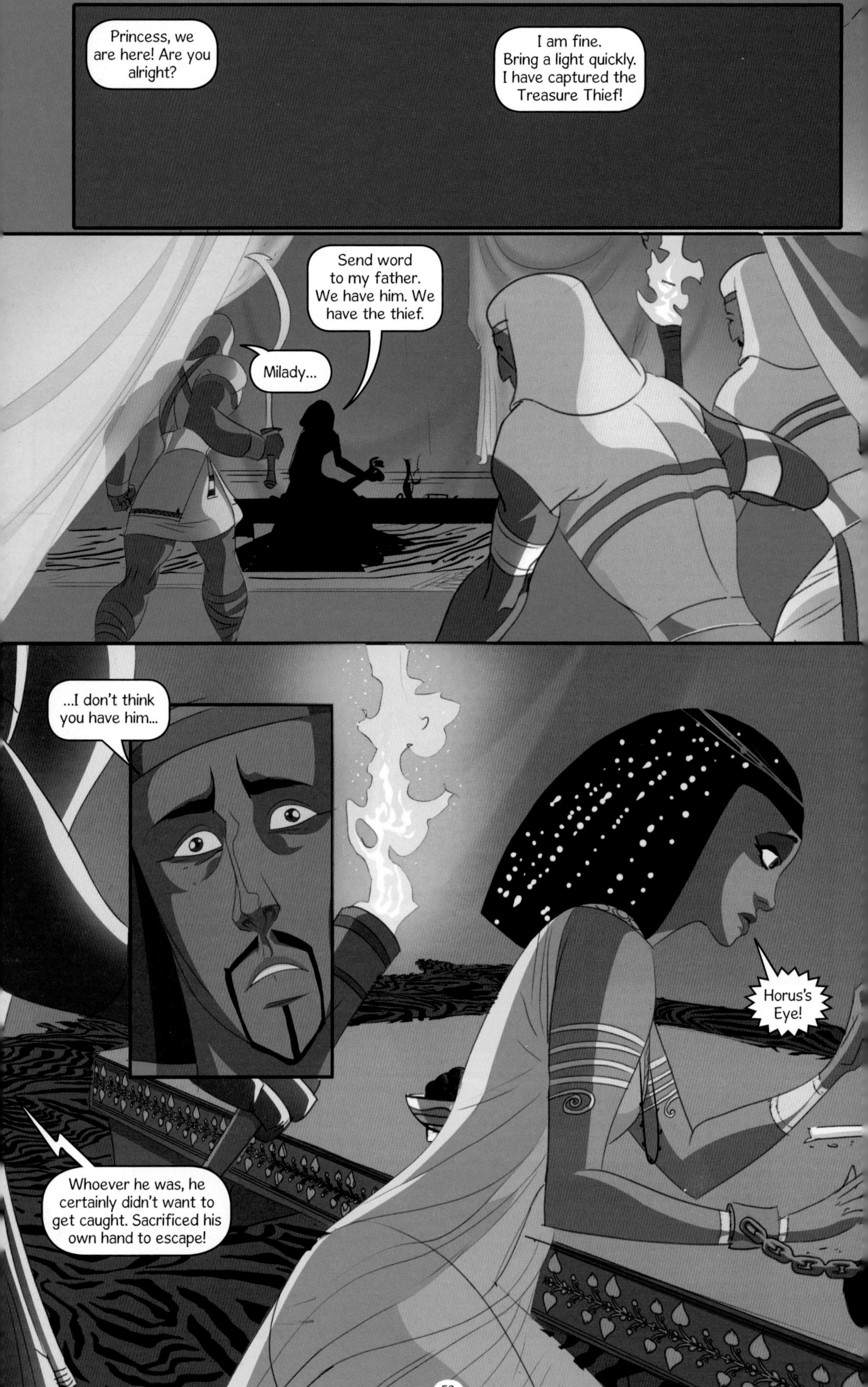
Princess, we are here! Are you alright?
I am fine. Bring a light quickly. I have captured the Treasure Thief!
Send word to my father. We have him. We have the thief.
Milady...
...I don't think you have him...
Horus's Eye!
Whoever he was, he certainly didn't want to get caught. Sacrificed his own hand to escape!

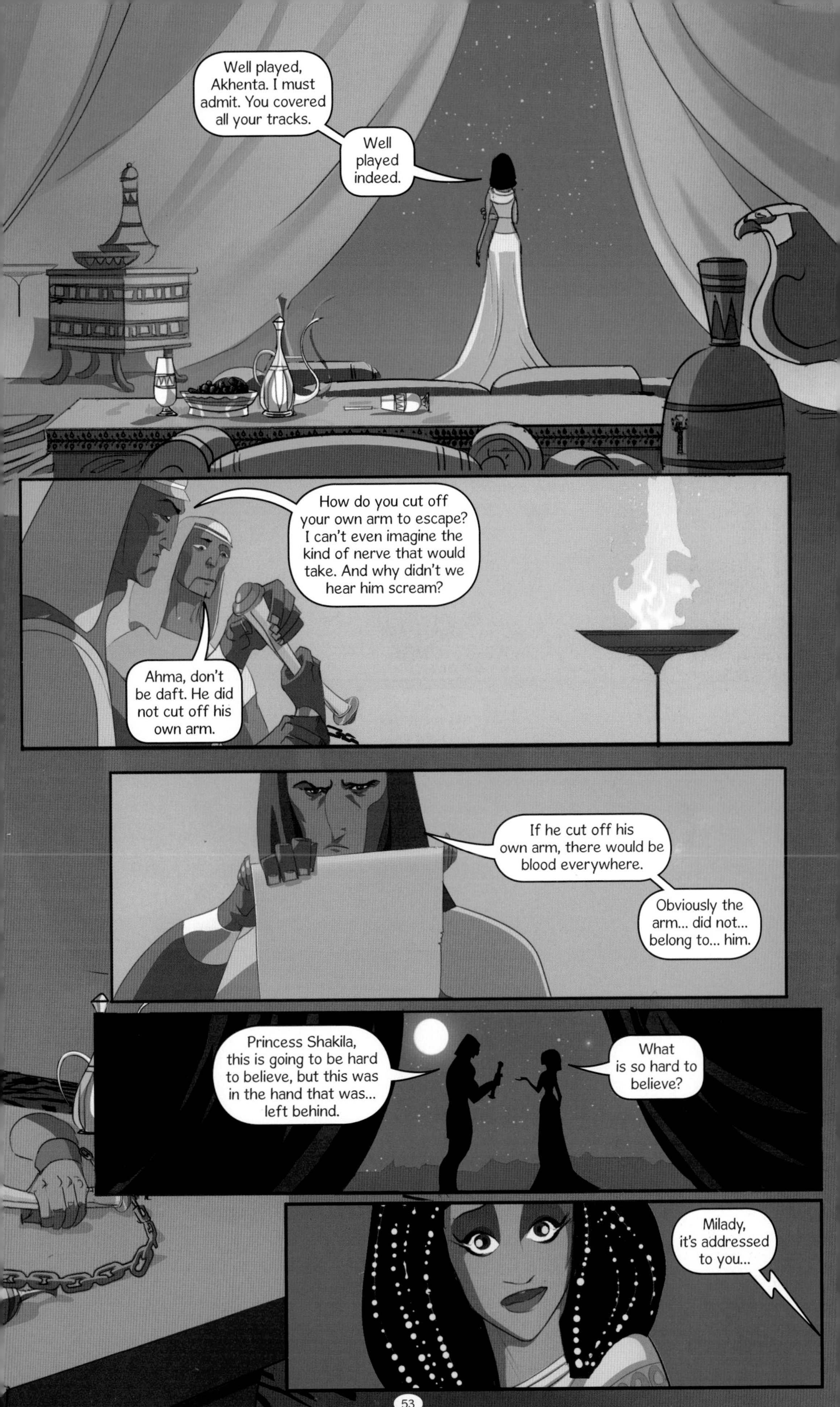
Well played, Akhenta. I must admit. You covered all your tracks.
Well played indeed.
How do you cut off your own arm to escape? I can't even imagine the kind of nerve that would take. And why didn't we hear him scream?
Ahma, don't be daft. He did not cut off his own arm.
If he cut off his own arm, there would be blood everywhere.
Obviously the arm... did not... belong to... him.
Princess Shakila, this is going to be hard to believe, but this was in the hand that was... left behind.
What is so hard to believe?
Milady, it's addressed to you...

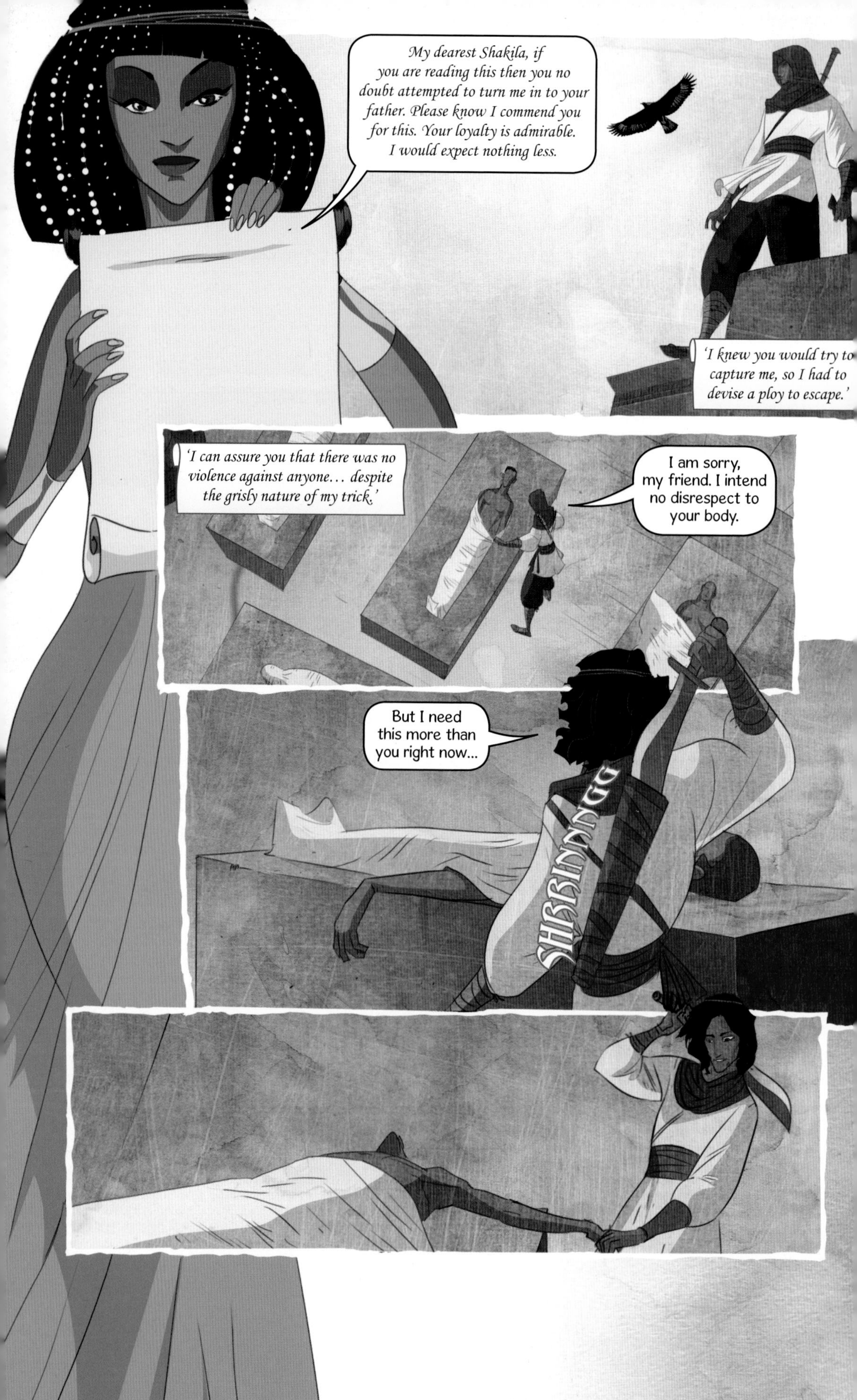
My dearest Shakila, if you are reading this then you no doubt attempted to turn me in to your father. Please know I commend you for this. Your loyalty is admirable. I would expect nothing less.
'I knew you would try to capture me, so I had to devise a ploy to escape.'
'I can assure you that there was no violence against anyone… despite the grisly nature of my trick.'
I am sorry, my friend. I intend no disrespect to your body.
But I need this more than you right now...
SHRRINNGG

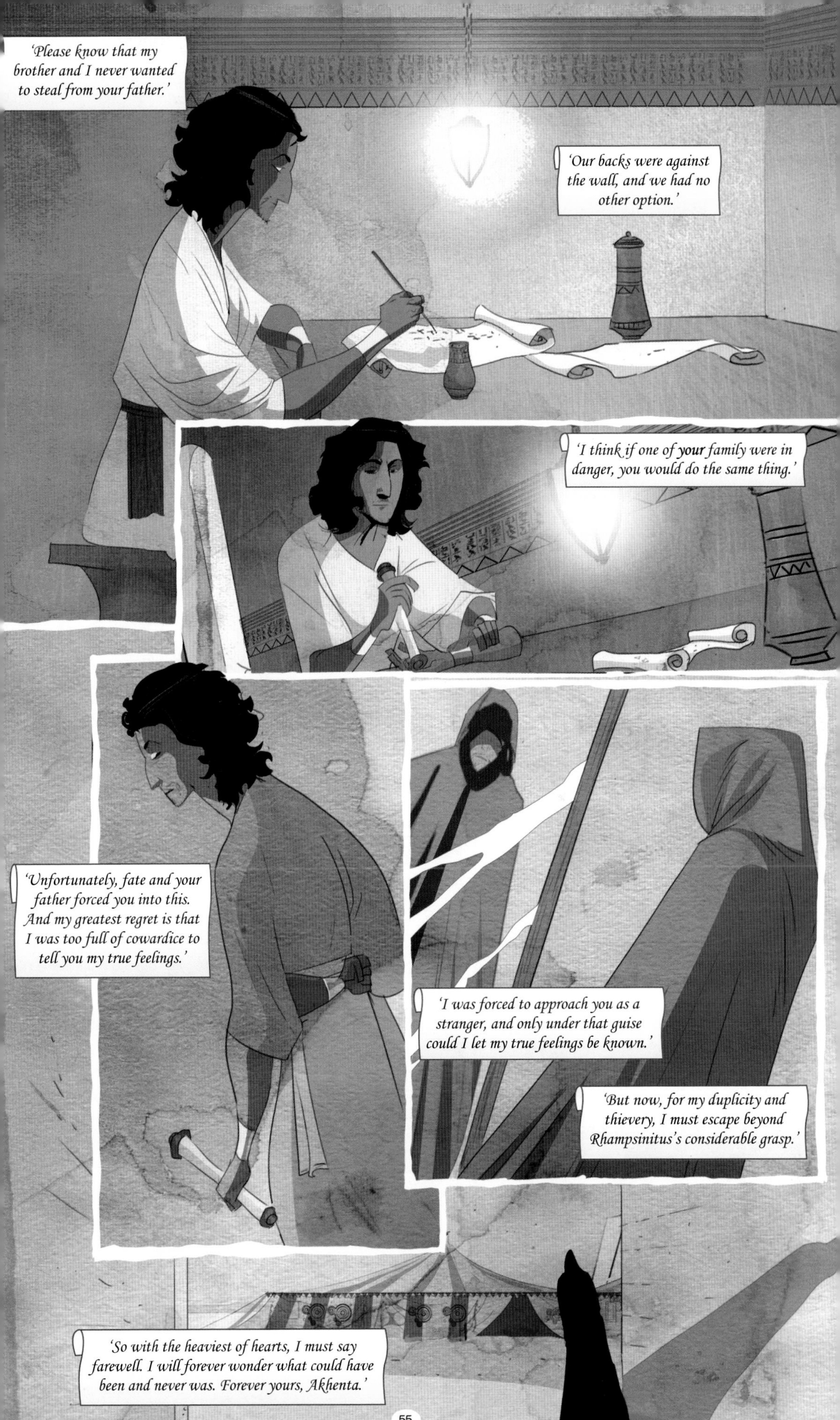
'Please know that my brother and I never wanted to steal from your father.'
'Our backs were against the wall, and we had no other option.'
'I think if one of **your** family were in danger, you would do the same thing.'
'Unfortunately, fate and your father forced you into this. And my greatest regret is that I was too full of cowardice to tell you my true feelings.'
'I was forced to approach you as a stranger, and only under that guise could I let my true feelings be known.'
'But now, for my duplicity and thievery, I must escape beyond Rhampsinitus's considerable grasp.'
'So with the heaviest of hearts, I must say farewell. I will forever wonder what could have been and never was. Forever yours, Akhenta.'

Shakila returned to her father's palace, eager to share the news of her discovery.

Father! Father, I must speak with you.

I have found your Treasure Thief, but he is not some greedy pilfering rogue.

He is much, much more...

The pharaoh listened to his daughter with rapt attention as she narrated the whole tale of the Treasure Thief.

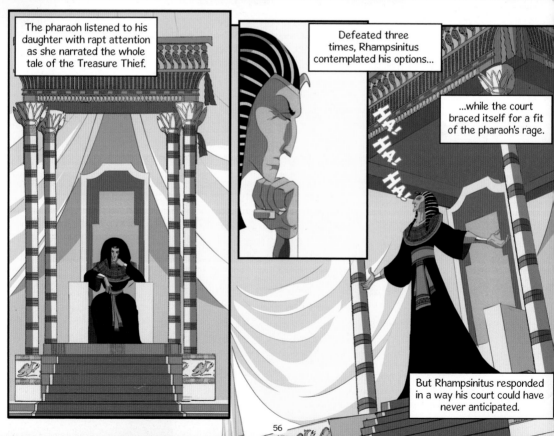

Defeated three times, Rhampsinitus contemplated his options...

...while the court braced itself for a fit of the pharaoh's rage.

HA! HA! HA!

But Rhampsinitus responded in a way his court could have never anticipated.

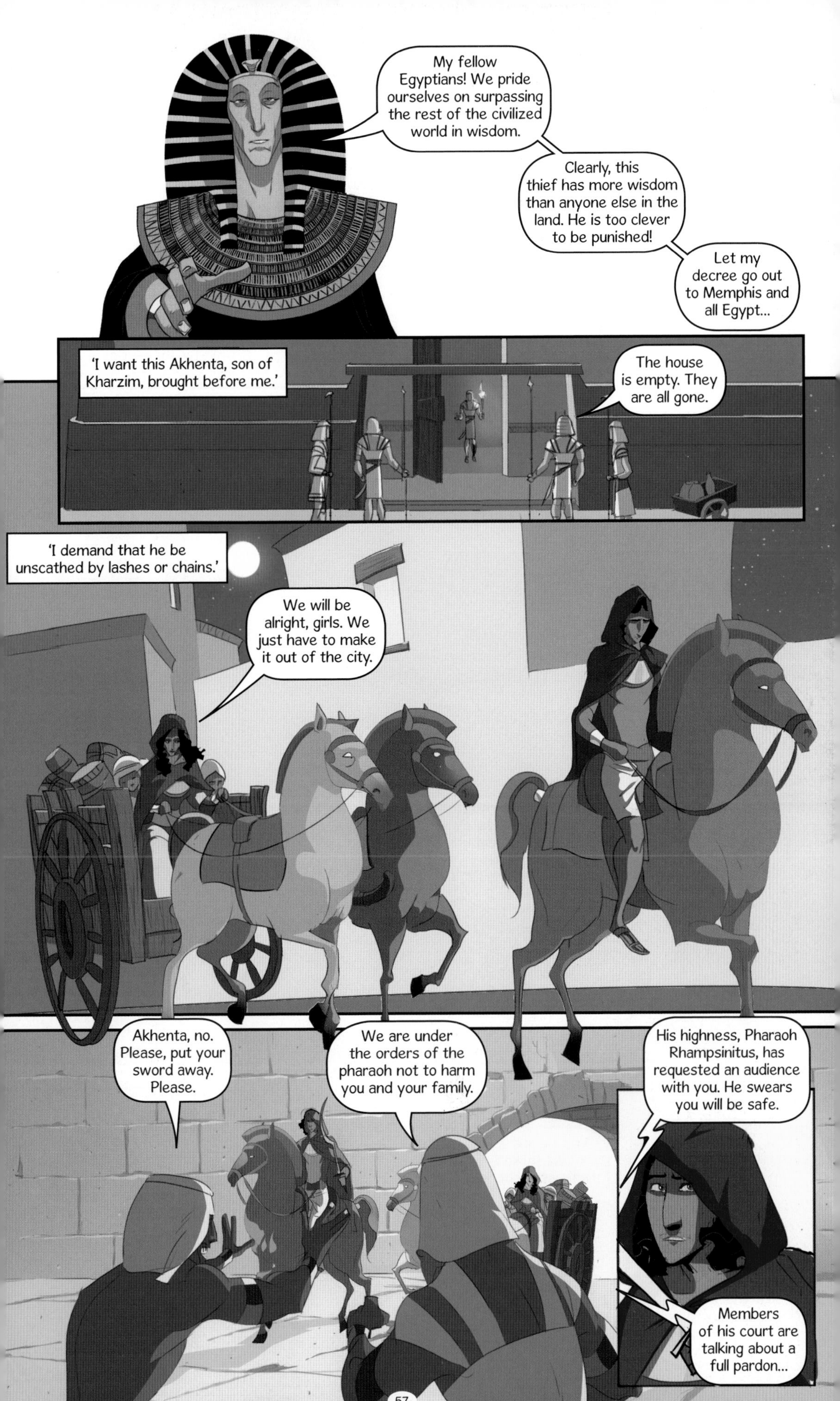
My fellow Egyptians! We pride ourselves on surpassing the rest of the civilized world in wisdom.
Clearly, this thief has more wisdom than anyone else in the land. He is too clever to be punished!
Let my decree go out to Memphis and all Egypt...
'I want this Akhenta, son of Kharzim, brought before me.'
The house is empty. They are all gone.
'I demand that he be unscathed by lashes or chains.'
We will be alright, girls. We just have to make it out of the city.
Akhenta, no. Please, put your sword away. Please.
We are under the orders of the pharaoh not to harm you and your family.
His highness, Pharaoh Rhampsinitus, has requested an audience with you. He swears you will be safe.
Members of his court are talking about a full pardon...

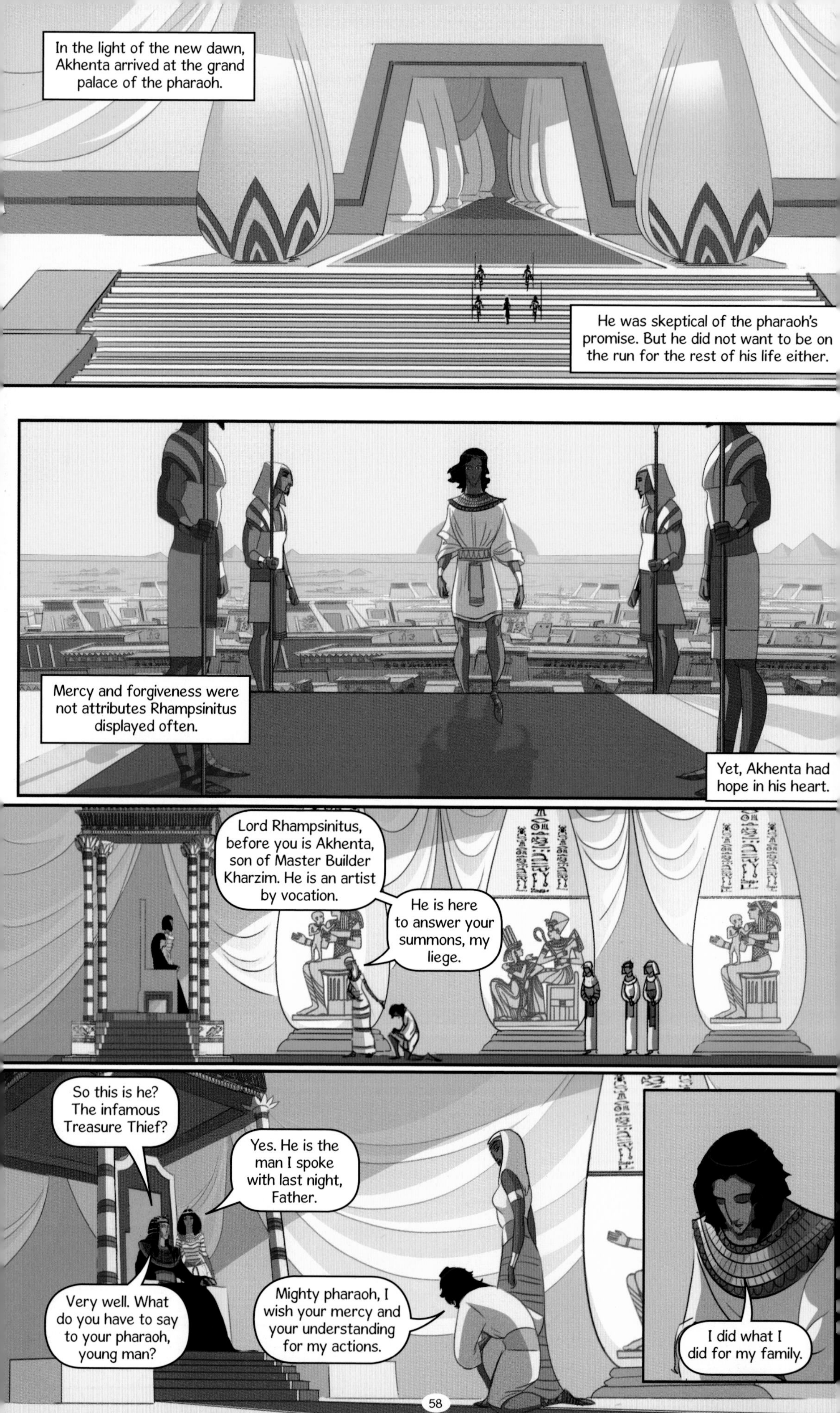
In the light of the new dawn, Akhenta arrived at the grand palace of the pharaoh.
He was skeptical of the pharaoh's promise. But he did not want to be on the run for the rest of his life either.
Mercy and forgiveness were not attributes Rhampsinitus displayed often.
Yet, Akhenta had hope in his heart.
Lord Rhampsinitus, before you is Akhenta, son of Master Builder Kharzim. He is an artist by vocation.
He is here to answer your summons, my liege.
So this is he? The infamous Treasure Thief?
Yes. He is the man I spoke with last night, Father.
Very well. What do you have to say to your pharaoh, young man?
Mighty pharaoh, I wish your mercy and your understanding for my actions.
I did what I did for my family.

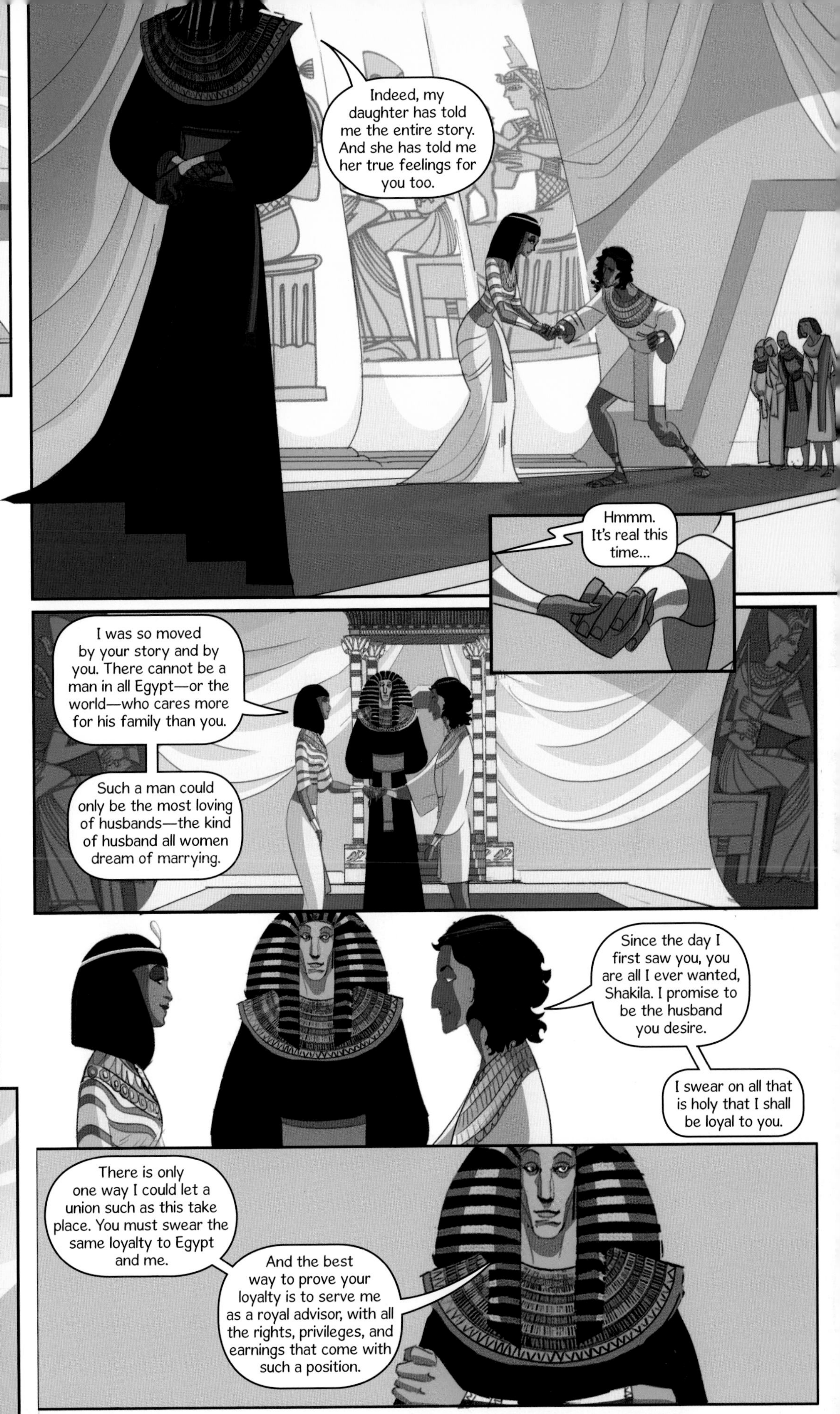
Indeed, my daughter has told me the entire story. And she has told me her true feelings for you too.
Hmmm. It's real this time...
I was so moved by your story and by you. There cannot be a man in all Egypt—or the world—who cares more for his family than you.
Such a man could only be the most loving of husbands—the kind of husband all women dream of marrying.
Since the day I first saw you, you are all I ever wanted, Shakila. I promise to be the husband you desire.
I swear on all that is holy that I shall be loyal to you.
There is only one way I could let a union such as this take place. You must swear the same loyalty to Egypt and me.
And the best way to prove your loyalty is to serve me as a royal advisor, with all the rights, privileges, and earnings that come with such a position.

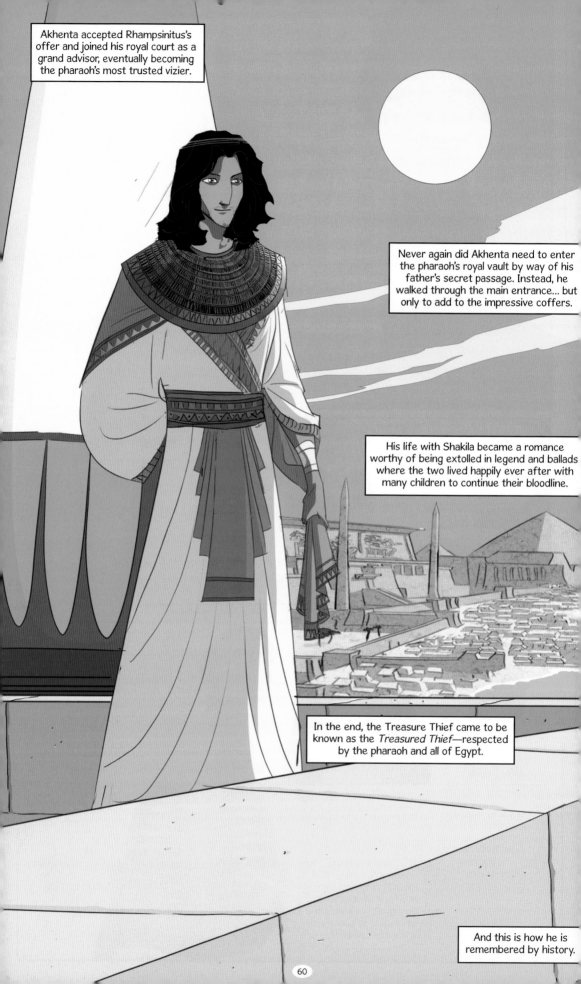

Akhenta accepted Rhampsinitus's offer and joined his royal court as a grand advisor, eventually becoming the pharaoh's most trusted vizier.

Never again did Akhenta need to enter the pharaoh's royal vault by way of his father's secret passage. Instead, he walked through the main entrance... but only to add to the impressive coffers.

His life with Shakila became a romance worthy of being extolled in legend and ballads where the two lived happily ever after with many children to continue their bloodline.

In the end, the Treasure Thief came to be known as the *Treasured Thief*—respected by the pharaoh and all of Egypt.

And this is how he is remembered by history.

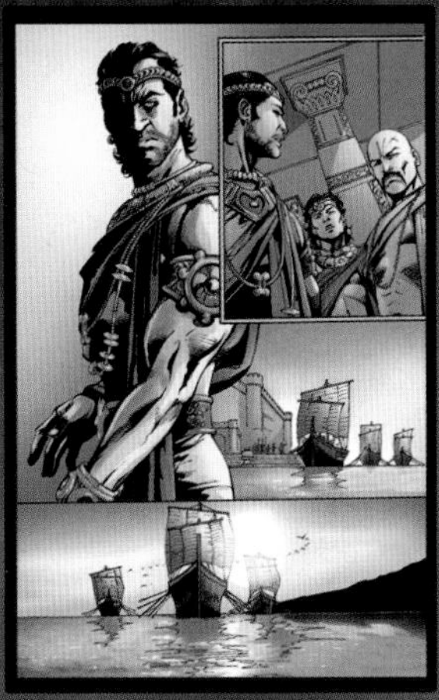

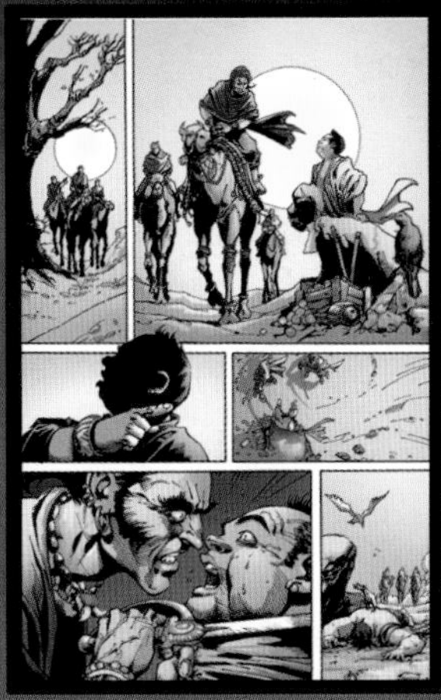

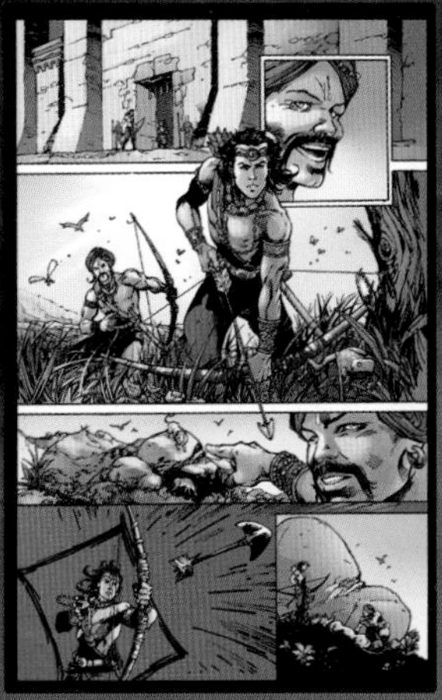

A brilliant and insightful recreation of the times of the Indus Valley Civilization.

Four times the size of its more famous contemporaries, the Indus Valley Civilization grew around a network of five great cities where peace and prosperity reigned. Prince Meluha, the young crown prince of Dholavira, enjoyed a life of luxury until Sargon, the ambitious ruler of the Mesopotamian city of Akkad, turned his eye toward the East and sent his army to take those lands.

Will Prince Meluha be able to save his kingdom? Or will the powerful Akkadians and their fearsome weapons of mass destruction destroy all before help is at hand?

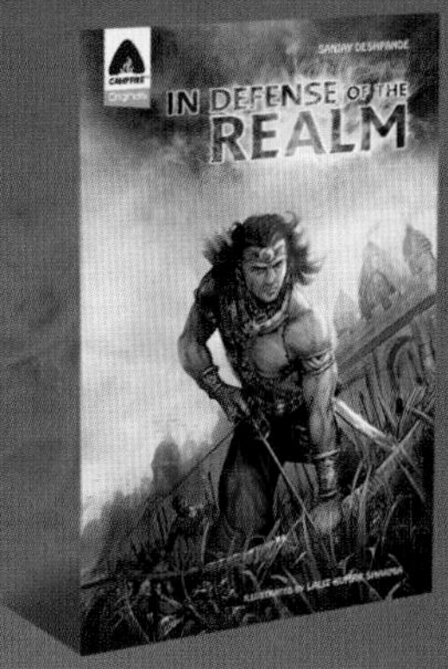
SANJAY DESHPANDE
IN DEFENSE OF THE REALM

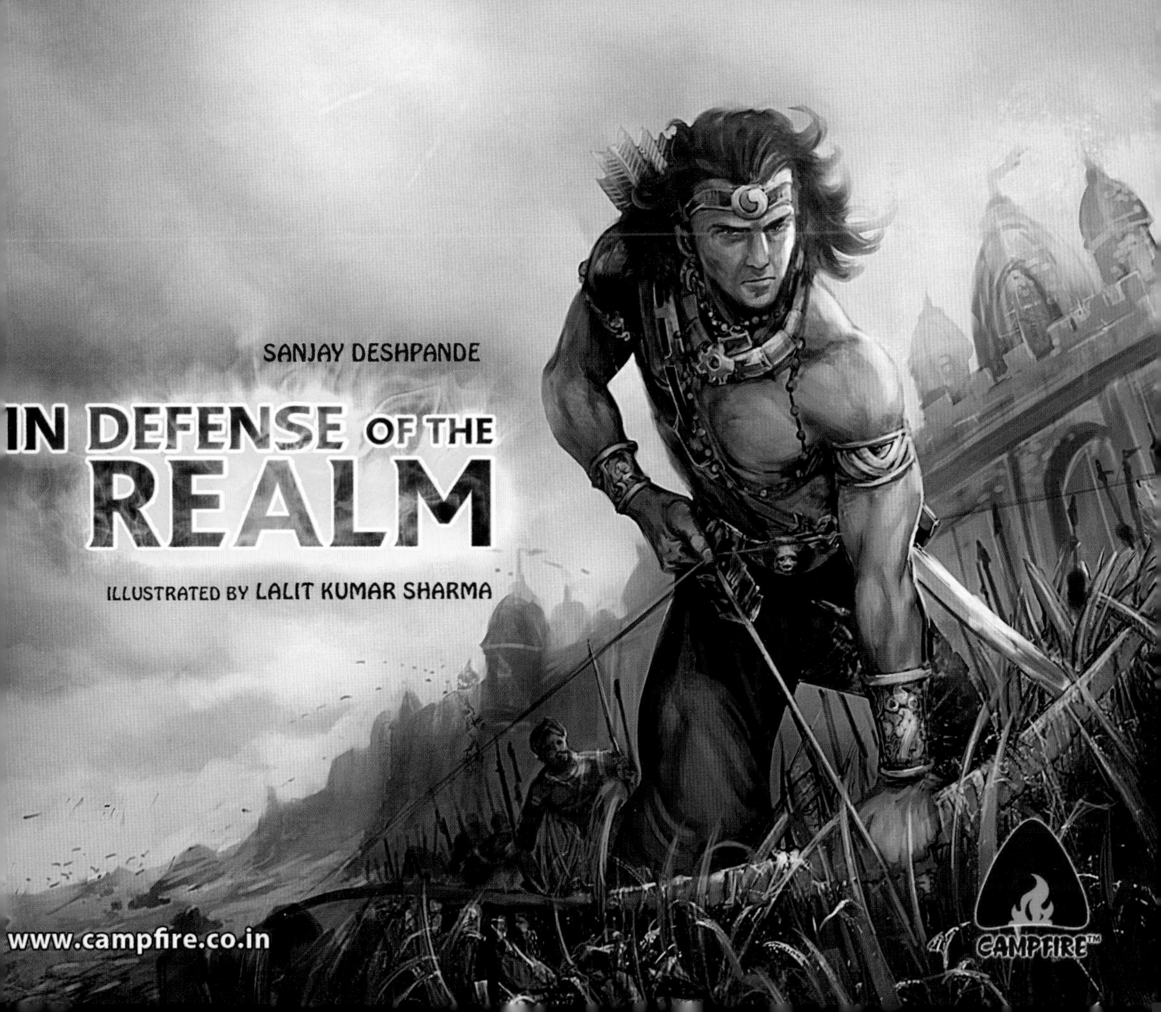
SANJAY DESHPANDE
IN DEFENSE OF THE REALM
ILLUSTRATED BY LALIT KUMAR SHARMA
www.campfire.co.in
CAMPFIRE™

STICKY FINGERS : ALL ABOUT THIEVES

MONA LISA MISSING!

It was the world's greatest art theft. On August 21, 1911, Vincenzo Peruggia, a carpenter at the Louvre Museum in Paris hid Leonardo da Vinci's *Mona Lisa* under his clothes, and escaped. Nobody even realized that it had been stolen until the next day! The Louvre was immediately shut down, the French border sealed, and all ships and trains searched. Even Pablo Picasso, the great painter, was questioned! But not a clue was found. People lined up just to see the empty spot where the painting once hung. Detectives searched for the painting for more than two years. In November 1913, Peruggia was arrested when he attempted to sell the painting to the directors of the Uffizi Gallery in Florence, Italy. The painting was returned to the Louvre, and the thief sentenced to six months of imprisonment.

THE DISAPPEARING DAREDEVIL

This incredible affair is something straight out of a James Bond movie! On November 24, 1971, an unidentified man referred to as Dan Cooper boarded a Boeing 727 aircraft from Portland to Seattle in the US. He threatened to blow up the plane unless he was given $200,000 and four parachutes. He collected the money, let the passengers go and, believe it or not, parachuted right out of the plane and was never seen again—alive or dead! Jet fighters following the plane never noticed him leap out, as it was raining hard. In 1980 a boy found around $6,000 of the ransom money on the banks of the Columbia River. But what happened to the man? Is he alive or did he die? Nobody knows till today, and the search is still going on.

THE PYRAMIDS OF GIZA

The Ancient Egyptians believed in the afterlife as we read in the story. So it was extremely important to protect and preserve the bodies of their kings entombed in the pyramids. The insides of the pyramids were like mazes with secret doors, booby traps, and dead-end passages. A decoy room filled with a few items would be made to fool thieves, while the actual burial chamber would be well hidden. There are many secret passages inside the great Pyramids of Giza. Most of them were sealed and plastered, so that no one would even realize that they existed. They were so narrow that one could just manage to squeeze one's body through, but would not be able to bring anything out from there.

THE GREAT TRAIN ROBBERY

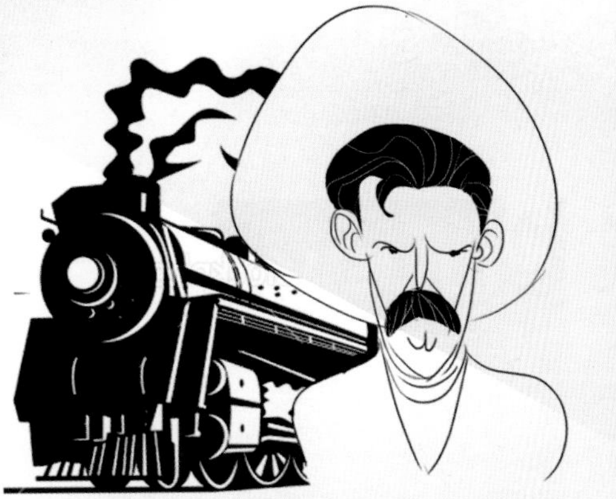

Robbers, prison escapes, and plastic surgery—The Great Train Robbery has it all! On August 8, 1963, in Buckinghamshire in England, fifteen robbers robbed a mail train and escaped with £2,600,000. Their fingerprints were later found on a catsup bottle and a Monopoly game board at an old farm house where they had hidden, and twelve men were caught. But Ronnie Biggs, one of the robbers, escaped from prison in a furniture van and became a notorious fugitive. He changed his looks with plastic surgery and fled to Brazil. The police did not find him until he finally surrendered in 2001. Today, you can find the famous Monopoly game board, which gave the robbers away, on display at the Thames Valley Police Museum.

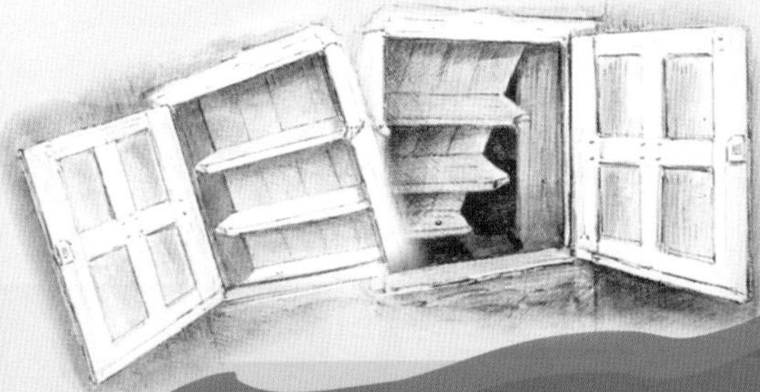

PRIEST HOLES

During the reign of Queen Elizabeth I in 16th century England, Catholic priests were brutally harassed and they had to constantly hide from the Queen's men. So, many Catholic homes had secret chambers called priest holes for the priests to hide in—behind fireplaces, walls, and under floors and stairs. Search parties would search for days while the poor priest would lie hidden right under their feet—cramped and sore! The Jesuit brother, Nicholas Owen or 'Little John' built many such hiding places. He even built a secret hiding place in a sewer, which you could reach by sliding down the toilet! You can find these hidey-holes in some old houses in England even today.

DID YOU KNOW?

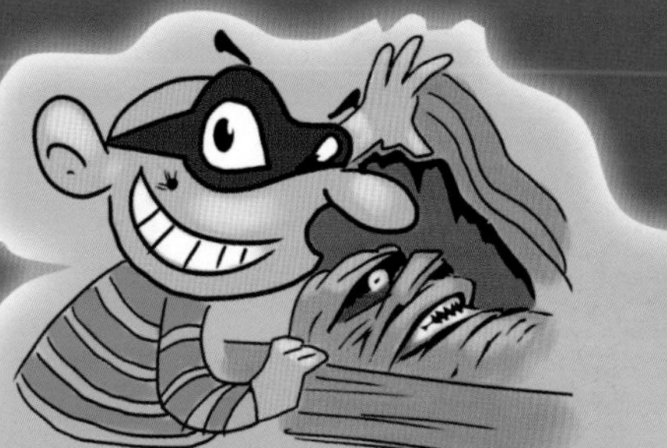

Tomb raiders, or tomb robbers, flourished in Ancient Egypt. Pyramids were tempting places for robbers, and they took great risks to break into them. Not even mummies were safe—the tomb robbers smashed coffins, and cut through layers of wrappings to get at jewelry and amulets. Tomb robbery was a major crime in Ancient Egypt and the guilty were put to death.

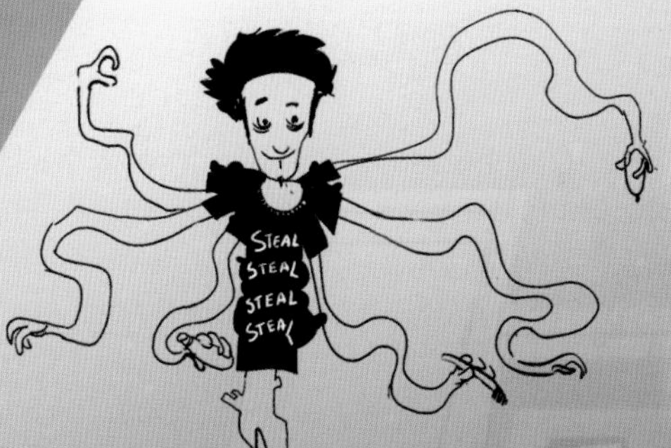
STEAL
STEAL
STEAL
STEAL

Kleptomania is an irresistible urge to steal. People with this disorder are compelled to steal things—usually objects they don't even need or are of little or no value!

You may also like to read other

titles from our **ORIGINALS SERIES**

Sidney Williams
Mark Jones
THE DUSK SOCIETY
ILLUSTRATED BY NARESH KUMAR

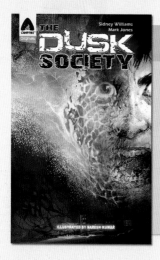

THE DUSK SOCIETY

In the hands of the newest recruits of The Dusk Society lies the fate of the world. Under the leadership of an evil man named Pierceblood, a whole host of terrifying monsters, including Count Dracula and Doctor Frankenstein, are getting ready to destroy the world. A secret organization created after World War I, The Dusk Society has to ensure that ancient, magical weapons do not fall into the wrong hands. Will they be able to stop Pierceblood's evil plan and save the world?

ALI BABA AND THE FORTY THIEVES RELOADED

In the reloaded version of the story of Ali Baba and the Forty Thieves, the world of Arabian Nights gives way to modern day Mumbai—the men wear suits and carry guns; their chosen steed has wheels instead of legs. An honest and hardworking auto rickshaw driver, Ali Baba's life is far from perfect. A chaotic sequence of events leads him, and a gang of forty thieves, on a merry chase through the suburbs of a modern metropolis. See how the turn of events, a few good friends, and presence of mind delivers Ali Baba from the most impossible of situations.

Ali Baba and the Forty Thieves
RELOADED
ILLUSTRATED BY AMIT TAYAL

LEWIS HELFAND
PHOTO BOOTH
Illustrated by
SACHIN NAGAR

PHOTO BOOTH

A deadly drug is about to flood the streets of New York City. The police has no leads on who is producing the drug, or where it is coming from. As far as Praveer Rajani, a ruthless Interpol agent, is concerned, the only way to prevent countless deaths lies in a handful of mysterious photographs. In the photographs, Praveer can see images of places that he has never known, and people he has long forgotten. But the photographs hold much more than clues to find the culprits—they carry the answers to the mystery of his own life!